Faith

Is A
Three-Legged
Stool

Patrick McWhorter

Published by

CHRISTIAN DAY
Publishing   Co.   ™

Published by Christian Day Publishing Company
6148 Jones Road, Flowery Branch, GA 30542

ISBN: 0982748604
ISBN-13: 978-0-9827486-0-2

Printed in the United States of America
2015 - Second Edition

And if I have the gift of prophecy, and know all mysteries and all knowledge; and if I have all faith, so as to remove mountains, but have not love, I am nothing.

I Corinthians 13:2

(American Standard Version)

CONTENTS

Is your faith genuine?

Is it weak faith, little faith, great faith, perfect faith or, as James described, dead faith?

Faith is your means of pleasing God.

Not only *can* you know whether your faith is pleasing to Him, you *must* know. You must not accept anything less than genuine faith, which comes directly from the Word of God as taught by the Holy Spirit. No other way exists to have genuine faith.

And what is that genuine faith? Simple belief, as so many people presume? Or is there more to faith than today's understanding of what it means to believe?

Mere presumption of truth comes when we accept the religious teachings and philosophies of men without making sure that what we've heard agrees with scripture and has the Holy Spirit's confirmation.

Genuine faith requires the heart of a child to grasp it. If you use grown-up logic to understand it, you might miss it.

May this book fire your love for God's truth and assure you of obtaining and maintaining genuine faith!

ACKNOWLEDGMENTS

This book has been stirring about in me for several years, having to take a back seat to my passion for writing in other genres. But the Lord has been patient with me, allowing me to see that my goals are only truly important as they mirror His plans.

He brought few encouragers as I got this manuscript in readable form. I began along the normal route of seeking the interest of publishing industry professionals and the comments of full-time ministers, but before long the Lord showed me that His direction and approval were the only confirmations I needed to proceed with the book.

On reading my first draft, my wife, Laurie, was the first person to wave the green flag by speaking five words. "This is an important book," she said. She is not given to hyperbole. Thank you, Laurie.

Above all, I give thanks to the Lord for allowing me to have a part in this project with Him.

The author

PREFACE

Patrick McWhorter is a layman. He has a degree in Journalism.

The thing that qualifies this writer, in the normal human sense of qualification, to write this book is that when Jesus died, the veil separating the Holy of Holies from the rest of the temple of God was rent and the Holy Spirit, at the appointed time, made a dwelling place in this writer's heart.

By the same means, the way into the presence of God was opened to all followers of Christ, even to former sinners of the Gentile persuasion, no longer just to the high priest in Judaism.

Is that a small thing?

No, it is the greatest event in the history of mankind!

Greater than possession of any degree. Greater than letters after one's name.

As great and uplifting as it is to receive instruction from knowledgeable and dedicated men and women of God, it can be in vain without the understanding that comes by the Holy Spirit of God. To have the Holy Spirit as Teacher is far superior to sitting under the tutelage of any revered and lettered gathering of credentialed faculty members of which any university might conceivably boast.

Yet, of course, this author claims no special favor in being taught by the Holy Spirit, for all believers have the same privilege to be so taught.

However, he believes that this book contains an aspect of Biblical understanding that has been largely overlooked in the foundational doctrines held by many in American Christianity.

The author has the temerity to believe God has commissioned him to make clear a single, seemingly small point about the nature of faith.

He thinks that small point is important enough for a book.

And he thinks the direction of the Holy Spirit is qualification enough.

So please overlook the fact that this preface does not present a long list of the author's achievements. As you read, imagine that you have seen and heard this writer numerous times over many years, if that will help you accept the authority of the Word of God administered under his stewardship.

Thank you for picking up this book.

May God use it to improve your understanding of faith. Or, if your understanding is already perfectly clear, may this book find its way through you into the hands of someone who needs a greater understanding of genuine faith. In fact, many "someones."

INTRODUCTION

Why would anyone write – or read, for that matter – a book defining faith?

Simply because many people need to understand faith more intimately.

Surely many of us who are God's children do have a firm grasp of what faith is through the teaching and correction of the Holy Spirit.

But just as surely, others do not.

God said about certain of His children, "*I will hide my face from them, I will see what their end shall be: for they are a very froward generation, children in whom is no faith.*" (Deuteronomy 32:19-20)

While some may have great faith, others may have weak faith, and some, little faith. We learn from James that some who hope or think they are God's children may even have dead faith. Paul commended Timothy on showing forth unfeigned or sincere faith, which clearly implies the existence, conversely, of insincere or non-genuine faith. Further, we see in scripture the antithesis of genuine faith:

"*I declare unto you the gospel which I preached unto you, which also ye have received, and wherein ye stand; By which also ye are saved, if ye keep in memory what I preached unto you, unless ye have believed in vain.*" I Corinthians 15:1-2

As a believer in Jesus Christ, you do not want to dwell in any kind or degree of faith that is vain or not genuine and not optimally effective. We need the strongest and most effective faith possible.

This book is for those who (A) don't really know how strong or weak their faith may be, (B) who do not yet have a sound grasp of faith, or (C) realize their current faith may be lacking something, and who (D) desire to have great faith.

Even if you consider your grasp of faith to be sound, do not stop reading. Instead, pray for deeper understanding, especially that you might be able to share truth with others. As you will see, this book is not written for the purpose of bringing condemnation or guilt upon anyone, but with the hope of increasing and improving your faith and correcting any misconceptions about faith that might exist.

To that end, I pray that no one reading this book will take offense at finding himself or herself falling short of the faith described herein, but will, instead, seek wholeheartedly to have God redirect his heart to embrace a strong, genuine Biblical faith in Jesus Christ, a faith that can and will withstand the inevitable trials intended to purify it for His glory.

In these last days, believers must be able to recognize the difference between true faith and false faith, and assist others to grasp the former. The Bible says, *"Without faith it is impossible to please God."* It should be obvious that false prophets, false teachers and false christs have false faith, that is, a faith that is not pleasing to God. Jesus said in Matthew 24 that *"there shall arise false Christs, and false prophets, and shall show great signs and wonders; so as to lead astray, if possible, even the elect."* (v. 24, ASV)

We are told to know those who labor among us. (I Thessalonians 5:12) That injunction does not mean to have a superficial acquaintance. We should know them well enough to know whether they walk by true faith or false faith.

If we look only to signs and wonders as proof that someone is a genuine follower of Christ, we might be led astray, for we know that signs and wonders can come from false as well as from true followers. So our understanding of faith must enable us to discern the difference. We must be able to avoid even the slightest deceptions brought by the enemy of our souls!

Even if you are one who knows intuitively what faith means, you need to know how to explain it to those who do not, especially to rear your children and disciple others in genuine faith. The odds are very high that you know someone who has a shallow understanding of faith.

Without doubt, many rely on platitudes, oversimplified definitions, traditional thinking or on a single scripture to define faith for them.

These people might consider faith such a simple concept that no one could misunderstand it. After all, faith is fundamental to Christianity. And many have been taught that faith is simple.

One person might say, Faith means simply believing.

Another might insist, No, it means trusting God.

Still others quote the writer of the book of Hebrews, *"Faith is the substance of things hoped for, the evidence of things not seen."*

Certainly, belief, trust, the evidence of things not seen – these are aspects of faith. And faith is nothing without a vital, committed relationship with God through Jesus Christ. We could add other shades of meaning to faith, but individual, narrowly defined definitions cannot reflect the entirety of its meaning.

But wait, you say. The "substance-and-evidence" definition is right out of the Bible. Doesn't that settle the issue?

Let me explain this way. The Bible says God is love. But does the word *love* completely describe God? When it is applied to God, even that beautiful word needs much more explanation than the common human understanding of love can provide. Do you really suppose that one scripture is sufficient to describe God? Consider, too, the scripture that says He is light. If we tried to pick a single scripture to gain some understanding of God, we would be very disadvantaged. Even many scriptures revealing aspects of His being are insufficient to define Him.

It is also true that no single scripture can adequately define faith.

If simple belief were a definition of faith sufficient to satisfy God's requirement for salvation and effective ministry to others, we would have needed approximately one paragraph of scripture to bring us into right relationship with God through Jesus Christ. We certainly would not need teachers. And really, would we need to consult the Holy Spirit for understanding? God could have raised up one scribe to describe the crucifixion and the resurrection, and He could have given us a one-sentence injunction: Accept what you have just read and you will be saved. Period. End of story.

It is certain that there are believers who are convinced that simple belief is all faith is, and they live their lives assuming that the concept only needs to fit into a tiny compartment in the back of their brains labeled, *Things I Believe* – the same category that covers data such as, *George Washington was the first president of the United States*. The Bible shows us examples of people who had a wrong understanding of God's terms for salvation, and reveals how serious such misunderstanding can be. (More on this later.)

The truth is, faith is too important to relegate to assumptions gleaned from our simple human understanding. We are told in Proverbs to *"lean not to your own understanding."* (3:5-6) Many false doctrines have come from relying on a human perspective to understand the things of God rather than relying on the Bible and the Holy Spirit. God said that doctrines originating in the commandments of men do not lead to true worship, but, in fact, counteract or negate attempts to worship Him. ("*But in vain do they worship me, teaching as their doctrines the precepts of men.*" Jesus quoted this scripture, Isaiah 29:13, in Matthew 15:9)

If we don't know the meaning of faith from *God's* perspective, all our efforts to be and to remain in right-standing with Him could be vain.

Because of this, I ask you to read on prayerfully. When you stop at or question something herein, take a moment to ask God to give you understanding. If what you have read is true, and you really seek to know truth, He will show you the truth of it. The key is to desire to know and love His truth, and to seek to apply it to your life, not merely to found your beliefs upon the doctrines and teachings given by men, including the things shared in this book.

This is a small book, but sufficient to correct any misconceptions about what Biblical faith truly is. The further aim and hope of this writing is to help move the various factions in the body of Christ closer together in our ability to exercise, in concert, the gift that God has dealt to all men: the measure of faith.

CHAPTER ONE

Are You Aiming at the Wrong "Faith"?

Think about one of the closing statements of the Introduction for a moment and realize how true it is: "If we don't know the meaning of faith from *God's* perspective, all our efforts to be and to remain in right-standing with Him could be vain."

Faith is so integral to salvation that if a person somehow fails to understand the definition as God parceled it out in scripture, his every effort at living and walking in faith could be misguided.

Sin is defined as missing the mark. Let me give you an analogy about faith that draws on that definition.

The importance of zeroing in on truth in the Bible might be demonstrated by the analogy of aiming a rifle at a target. If the target is one meter from the end of the barrel, your aim can be off by one degree and you will still hit very near the center of the target. But if the target is one-quarter mile away, one degree in miscalculation will cause you to miss the target by about 23 feet. The element of distance is of fundamental importance to accuracy in aiming a rifle. The greater the distance, the more critical the aim.

But we're not talking about physical distance, of course, when we're talking about truth. We are talking about fundamental importance and, consequently, spiritual distance. The importance of faith in the subject of salvation is absolutely crucial, far more important than peripheral questions such as whether we should play musical instruments when we worship or if we should meet in homes or in steepled buildings. After all, Paul told us that "whatever is not of faith is sin." (Romans 14:23)

Therefore, the more important the question regarding salvation, the more critical it is to our aim, so to speak, assuming we want to hit the center of the target of truth.

In Isaiah 55:8, God says, *"For my thoughts are not your thoughts, neither are your ways my ways."* We make dramatic errors when we try to force God's meaning into the mold of our own understanding. God expects us to do just the opposite – to adapt our understanding to His meaning – and, thereby, to be transformed by the renewing of our minds. (Romans 12:1-2)

When you are trying to hit a target of low importance, a minor miscalculation may turn out to be only a minor error in the grand scheme of things. But a seemingly minor error in the meaning of something as important as faith can result in a major miscalculation in terms of salvation because it is so fundamental to our following Jesus Christ. We can say this: the more important the goal, the more critical one's understanding of the most elemental factors in reaching the goal. Thus, it is of utmost importance to make no assumptions about faith, but, instead, to study it thoroughly.

What goal in God's Word is more important than salvation by grace? And what is more important in having this gracious salvation than the element of faith in Jesus Christ? In truth, if you miss the true meaning of faith, it will be far worse than being slightly off in your aim; it will be as if you were aiming at the wrong target all together. You will totally miss the mark.

Suppose NASA were as careless about space missions as some believers are about knowing the Word of God. A fraction of one degree miscalculation in course on a mission to Mars could be a multi-billion-dollar error. A comparable miscalculation in fundamental truth from the Bible can be far more costly than that!

Can you see, now, how essential our understanding of faith is?

There are many references to faith in the Bible, and the truth is that each contributes significant information about it – each provides a tick in the adjustment of our aim – so that no one scripture standing alone can encapsulate the meaning of faith.

As asserted before, without doubt, many believers have intuitively understood the definition of faith through the teaching of the Holy Spirit, and have practiced it diligently without feeling the need to dissect it. But we are called to make disciples. If our understanding of faith is only intuitive, how can we communicate the full meaning of it to someone who knows nothing of it? Or if it is in error, how can we make true disciples?

Now, I have suggested that many others through the ages have presumed to know what faith is, but missed it completely, perhaps even ignoring definitions altogether, assuming faith's meaning to be so superficial and near as a target that it required no aim or explanation, and thus, no attention – which, by the way, is exactly the kind of attitude that might lead to treating it lightly.

You might ask, How in the world could anyone know for certain that there are people who presumed to know what faith is and yet missed it altogether? The only way to know that is through God's Word.

In the book of Matthew, chapter seven, Jesus reveals that, "*Not every one that saith unto me, Lord, Lord, shall enter into the kingdom of heaven.*" On the day of God's judgment there will be those who are surprised to learn that they did not live in faith, despite their efforts. Jesus said there will be "many" of them. Matthew chapter 25 also shows that many whom God will classify as "goats" were apparently ignorant of what God had expected of them. The sheep and goats alike appeared to be somewhat surprised by the explanation Jesus gave for their hitting or missing the mark of genuine faith.

Some of those Jesus described *thought* they were living by faith in God and were performing works that they presumed would please God. But they found out, too late, that they were wrong. The tragedy is, they could have found out the truth while they still had time to change!

Where in the world would misguided people get such wrong ideas about the truth in God's Word? Popular theology, no doubt. Cultural norms. Tradition.

But the most troubling source of all is in teachings within assemblies of the *Church*.

The clear indication of scripture is that many of the misguided are indeed in Christian church groups, acting and talking so much like everyone else that few suspect they are not actually followers of Jesus. No, not even they themselves are aware in some instances.

And therein lies the potential for the greatest tragedy of misunderstanding the world has ever known: people so close to salvation, yet so far away, and going basically unchallenged in their unbelief by believers focused in a different direction.

Those of us who accept the Great Commission of Jesus presume we know who to target when we go about fulfilling it. Oh, we may not profile, but we know where and how to find unbelievers. They may wear suits or saris. They may work in banks or bars. And they may live in gated communities or ghettos.

But they all have one thing in common: they don't "go to church."

Or so we suppose.

A failing of evangelical Christians seems to be that we see church attendance as a mark of rightness with God, as though Christ came to become the Roof over the Church instead of the Door into it.

Is that true? No, you say, evangelicals realize that not all unbelievers are unchurched.

Then how is it that we only typically reach out to the "unchurched"? We know there must be entire sects of people, even denominations, calling themselves believers who operate on another kind of faith than that described in the Bible, and we are content to let them alone because they might resent our correcting them.

Or perhaps something deeper stops us. Maybe we don't have full confidence in our own beliefs. If we did not receive our beliefs from the Holy Spirit, but took the word of men instead, then we will not have unshakeable confidence in the things we believe.

Let me dig a little deeper into our collective discomfort zone.

We evangelicals tend to agree that even in *our* midst – *in evangelical church groups* – we have believers in Christ who operate on an unscriptural kind of faith, and we don't bother to teach them what true faith is.

In many Christian congregations across America, it would be difficult to recognize a faulty faith because of the shallow level of involvement we tend to have in each others' lives and because of the compartmentalization of faith among believers today. Faith is typically an acceptable subject of conversation for Sundays between 11:00AM and noon, but taboo in the secular settings we inhabit the rest of the week.

In short, we often know absolutely nothing about the faith of other believers, even those with whom we attend Christian meetings, because our fellowship tends to be socially oriented, even secular, and our faith dependent upon human-devised solutions. We give our faith in God's Word little opportunity for practical expression in daily life.

Are we willing to have those sitting next to us in church meetings turn out to be among the "many" who are surprised when they are rejected by God for a false understanding of faith? For that matter, are we ourselves willing to be among that number?

We must seek out the lost, whether outside church walls or inside, and give them the truth. But we must first have it to give.

In the arena of faith, scriptural truth is the starting point and the ending point. In other words, the Holy Bible – not the Koran or any other pretender to holy writ – comprises the only grounds for what is true. And as much as you may not like this, it is true: the

Holy Spirit is the only Instructor you need to explain the words of scripture.

Christian ministers – pastors, teachers, evangelists, etc. – may swallow hard upon reading that last statement because some may think they have the sole or primary responsibility to teach us. They do not. They have the responsibility to receive the words of truth directly from the Word of God, and their understanding of that truth directly from, and only from, the Holy Spirit Himself. They have the responsibility to live, preach and teach what the Holy Spirit has shown them from God's Word, and will be held accountable for the truth of their teachings (See James 3:1).

But each individual believer also has the responsibility to submit to the teaching of the Holy Spirit! That is, no matter what we hear from human teachers, who may be flawed, we must get our understanding first and foremost from the Holy Spirit, who is not flawed.

This is not disrespect toward a pastor or teacher sharing the Word of God. And it must not be. On the contrary, it is a demonstration of greater respect toward the Holy Spirit. If you use this understanding as a means of displaying disrespect toward those God has raised up to teach and pastor, then you must deal with the inner resentment that leads to disrespect. The Church has too much division as it is, without the engendering of more.

The apostle John, speaking by the Holy Spirit, said it very plainly.

"But the anointing which ye have received of him abideth in you, and ye need not that any man teach you: but as the same anointing teacheth you of all things, and is truth, and is no lie, and even as it hath taught you, ye shall abide in him." 1 John 2:27

Some of us have listened to so many recorded messages from preachers the world around, read so many books by famous men and women, attended so many believers conferences, and heard espoused so many doctrines from the pulpit that we have developed a dullness of hearing, leaving us inattentive to and un-led by the Holy Spirit.

And some of us are simply lazy. We are so dependent on ministers spoon-feeding us doctrines that we could not follow the Holy Spirit if He wore a Day-Glo vest and carried a bull horn.

The apostle Paul learned to understand the scriptures directly from the Lord. He said in Galatians that he was not taught the meaning of the scriptures by humans.

"But I certify you, brethren, that the gospel which was preached of me is not after man. For I neither received it of man, neither was I taught it, but by the revelation of Jesus Christ." Galatians 1:11-12

Does that contradict other scriptures? As a young man, wasn't Paul taught at the feet of Gamaliel? Yes, he was taught the "Old Testament" law, which gave him a foundation of scripture God could use, but that merely shows us that the Word of God requires the teaching power of the Holy Spirit, Whom Paul (Saul) had not yet received when he was a youth. Knowing scripture did not prevent him from misunderstanding and misapplying it in the absence of the Holy Spirit's teaching. Paul goes on to say that when God called him to preach, he *"conferred not with flesh and blood."* (verse 16) He was led and taught by the Holy Spirit.

Some ministers take worldly wisdom and wrap it in Biblical texts to support their preconceived beliefs or to justify what they *hope* is true. Why? The same reason the rest of us have done it to some extent: we want to be spoon-fed; we want to trust the authoritative voice of man rather than be held accountable for obtaining truth directly from the Word of God as taught by the Holy Spirit. Safety in numbers? Perhaps. We are sheep-like creatures and want the safety of a flock. The problem with error is, there is no safety in numbers. Each of us is responsible to seek truth from God.

In the book, *The Heavenly Man*, written by a Chinese believer called Brother Yun, the author describes a time of heavy persecution by Chinese authorities against the underground church. As persecution increased, so did unity among and between groups of believers. Western Christian groups, knowing that Bibles were forbidden in China, began smuggling them into the country. For a time, Christianity grew and so did the hope and love of believers.

"However," said Brother Yun, "after a few years these same mission organizations started putting other books at the top of the bags of Bibles. These were books about one particular denomination's theology, or teaching that focused on certain aspects of God's Word. This, I believe, was the start of disunity among many of China's house churches." He said, "We read all these booklets and soon we were confused!"

The Word of God alone has all the instruction needed for the Christian life, and the Holy Spirit alone has all the power needed to teach it.

Now before I progress further, I think I hear the voices of some readers saying, But this is just one more book, and you are just one more preacher about to foist upon us one more doctrine!

Good! You are exhibiting signs of caution. Now here's what will keep you from making this just one more spoon-fed taste of scriptural pabulum:

Take what you read in this book and study it out in God's Word, and ask the Holy Spirit to tell you the truth of what you have read.

Is that a "cop-out" on the part of this author? No, because you are already solely responsible for searching out and discovering truth through the Word and the Holy Spirit. If you have grown lazy listening to sermons without bothering to search out the truth of what you hear, you will not like hearing that, but it is nevertheless true.

Even if you have believed false teachings rather than studying the Word of God for yourself to find the truth, God will still hold you responsible for error. Jesus said, *"Take heed that no man deceive you."* Who must take heed? You must. He has made it clear in His Word that the Holy Spirit is to be our Teacher. He is the only Teacher we can trust to bring us unadulterated truth. Therefore, it is individual believers who must take heed.

This book urges you to do just that, to listen to the Holy Spirit. Just be careful that you are fully submitted to Him, willing to hear the truth from His voice, and not holding an inner desire to keep as pets any "sacred cows" that might be grazing in your green pastures.

Paul called the Bereans "noble" because they did not simply accept every word he uttered, but *"searched the scriptures daily, whether those things were so."* Acts 17:10-11

Let me caution you to read with a love for the truth rather than with a love for <u>what you already believe</u>.

In 2 Thessalonians 2, Paul says of those deceived by the "man of perdition," that they perished *"because they received not the love of the truth, that they might be saved."* (v.10)

Hear what he is saying: "...*that they might be saved.*"
This scripture encapsulates a truth you could miss if
you read it lightly. And that is, love of truth is crucial
to salvation. (Read more about this in Chapter Four.)

Without a love for the truth, how can anyone be
saved? If your agenda in reading the Bible is to hold
on to and prop up what you already understand, not
even the Holy Spirit can teach you. You have become
unteachable. You are like the monkey whose fist is
caught in a trap because it is full of goods he is
unwilling to release.

I don't care if you are a minister of righteousness or a
rank sinner, if you will demand that your soul cherish,
seek and accept the truth regardless of what sacred
cows must fall in order to possess it, and stick with
that throughout your search of the Word of God,
asking the Holy Spirit of God to teach you, you will
find the truth.

Only the Holy Spirit can teach you anything of truth
and assure you that you won't be among the "many"
deceived whom God will reject in that terrible day.

Now is the moment to ask yourself, "Did I get all my
understanding from diligent study of the Word of God
and the teaching of the Holy Spirit, or did I receive my
understanding of critical, foundational elements from
men?"

If you left out the diligent personal study of the Word
of God with personal submission to the teaching

ministry of the Holy Spirit you may be standing on shaky ground spiritually. That would mean you depended upon the preaching of faulty men or on your own understanding, and have thereby nailed your hope for salvation on *man's* understanding of God and His Word, rather than on the faultless understanding and teaching of the Holy Spirit.

If you find that you have accepted teachings second-hand, go immediately to God and ask Him to fill you with a love and hunger for the truth that will spur your study and teachability. While error is a very bad thing, coming to realize you have opened yourself to it is a good thing, for with the realization can come the understanding of the exciting adventure of being taught by the Holy Spirit Himself.

Is it any wonder we have so many contradicting doctrines among Christians?

If you are like so many who are deceived, you will not be concerned about the differences in doctrines, because you will assume that your "group" or denomination is the one that is right.

Let me tell you quickly that I believe that sort of assumption could be the very reason the people Jesus described in Matthew 7:21-23 were shocked at being rejected by Christ.

Perhaps they took what they thought was the easy road to understanding – not searching out truth for themselves, but accepting what sounded reasonable to their own ears – and assumed they would be okay.

No man presently on earth has perfect understanding of the Bible. All of us have some degree of faulty understanding. Therefore, if we accept the teachings of men (or women, for that matter) without submitting them to the proof of the Holy Spirit and God's Word, we are susceptible to great error. Even if the teaching we hear from men is true, if we have not submitted it to the Holy Spirit through personal subjection to the Word of God, we will not personally "possess" the truth, but we will have, in essence, borrowed it. I believe the actual revealing of truth must come by the Holy Spirit, even if we hear it first from "flesh and blood." (See Mathew 16:17)

Do not opt for the lounge chair of second-hand faith. Get your understanding directly from the Source.

That is God's plan and intention to provide you and me with genuine faith rather than a cheaply obtained knock-off.

CHAPTER TWO

The Tragedy of Unsaved Believers

Unsaved believers?

Is that an oxymoron?

Not at all. Devils believe the gospel, says the writer of the book of James, and they tremble. (James 2:19) Many rulers in Jesus's day believed in Him, according to John 12:42-43, but would not confess Him as their Lord because *they loved the praise of men more than the praise of God.*" In fact, many people believe enough of the Bible to call themselves "believers" and Christians, but lack the fruit to verify they are "trees of righteousness."

I recall a study some years back that showed a high percentage of Americans – something like 75 percent – called themselves Christians. Responses deeper in the survey, however, revealed that only about 11 percent lived the kind of lifestyles that supported their claim.

If you claim to be a believer, I am unable to judge the truth of that statement, so I have to accept your word. I can judge some acts, whether they are the acts of a true believer according to the Word of God, but it is a fact that even true believers sometimes fail and commit sin. Only God is able to judge whether a person is a *bona fide* believer in Christ – and let me emphasize *in Christ* – for at times, even those exhibiting signs of being strong believers are deceived about their relationship to Him.

As mentioned in the Preface, the proof of the last part of that statement comes from the Bible. Take a look at the book of Matthew, chapter seven, and let's focus on verses 21 through 23:

"Not every one that saith unto me, 'Lord, Lord,' shall enter into the kingdom of heaven; but he that doeth the will of my Father which is in heaven. Many will say to me in that day, 'Lord, Lord, have we not prophesied in thy name? and in thy name have cast out devils? and in thy name done many wonderful works?' And then will I profess unto them, 'I never knew you: depart from me, ye that work iniquity.'"

Here, Jesus is referring to people who call Him "Lord." That fact alone does not necessarily peg these people as believers because, as you might have already considered, they could have decided instantly upon standing in judgment before Christ that it might be a beneficial tactic to refer to Him as Lord. However, the fact that they, in their lifetimes, did things that are certifiably the acts of strong believers, and moreover, did them in the name of Jesus, leaves little doubt that at least *they thought* they were believers. And if they thought they were believers, it is likely that others – their friends, neighbors, family members – thought of them as believers as well.

These people had the impression that their acts, done in Christ's name, were proof of their status as believers. Their plaintive tone in the scripture above, sounding very much like a defense, suggests that they were surprised to be thought of by Jesus as workers of iniquity. They expected to be welcomed into His kingdom.

The verses immediately prior to verse 21 have Jesus talking about false prophets, "*which come to you in sheep's clothing, but inwardly they are ravening wolves.*" It would be easy to suggest that verses 21 through 23 only refer to false prophets and not their victims, especially because the works they describe in verse 22 are works some typically ascribe to prophets – prophesying and casting out devils.* Yet in Matthew 24, Jesus reveals that the works of false prophets "*deceive many.*" (v. 11) So, whether the "many" referred to in verses 21 and 22 of chapter seven are the false prophets, their victims, or ordinary church-goers, it is clear that they are deceived. And further, while many ascribe those kinds of works to the duties of prophets, we actually see ordinary believers in the New Testament doing the same works. So the "many" of that scripture appears to fit believers who are "in the ministry" as well as those who are not.

The warning Jesus gives in Matthew 24:4 is, "*Take heed that no man deceive you.*" The direct inference is that you have control over your own heart, whether you are deceived or escape deception. Therefore, get truth for yourself and obey it, so you will not be deceived. According to James 1:22, the way we are to ensure we are not deceived is by being doers of the Word of God. ("*But be ye doers of the word, and not hearers only, deceiving your own selves.*")

This gives us insight into another of Jesus's comments in Matthew 7. Jesus said, "*Not every one that saith unto me, 'Lord, Lord,' shall enter into the kingdom of heaven; but he that doeth the will of my Father which is in heaven.*" We must be faithful to obey God's Word – to do His will – if we expect to remain undeceived, and to enter the kingdom of heaven.

But wait. Weren't the people of Matthew 7 obedient?

Take special note that the works claimed by the unfortunate people in 7:22 were the kind of works outwardly qualifying as "*the will of my Father.*"

"*...have we not prophesied in thy name? and in thy name have cast out devils? and in thy name done many wonderful works?*"

Jesus Himself cast out devils and prophesied. We see the apostles casting out devils and prophesying. And it's noteworthy to cite Mark 16:17, where Jesus said ordinary believers will cast out devils.

We have to conclude, then, that the acts the people of verse 22 performed were not the major issue with Jesus.

Let me repeat that: the people of Matthew 7:22 – who said, "*Lord, Lord, have we not prophesied in thy name? and in thy name have cast out devils? and in thy name done many wonderful works?"* – were rejected by Jesus for some reason other than whether they did or did not do the works listed. The works they claimed to have performed were good works, works that believers were and are expected to do.

Jesus's words in verse 21 show us two important things: (1) Just *calling* Him "Lord" means nothing relative to doing the will of God, and (2) just doing the acts He commands us to do in His name does not mean we are doing the will of the Father. In fact, the two together do not necessarily comprise *"the will of my Father."*

Doesn't that seem to contradict the common beliefs of many Christians you know? In fact, doesn't that seem to contradict the well known scripture in James 2:18, that says:

"Yea, a man may say, Thou hast faith, and I have works: shew me thy faith without thy works, and I will shew thee my faith by my works."

For that matter, does it not also seem to contradict the scripture in James 1:22, saying:

"But be ye doers of the word, and not hearers only, deceiving your own selves."

These two scriptures seem to be saying that "doing the works" prescribed by the Word of God is the key to completing your faith and protecting you from self-deceit. In fact, the people to whom Jesus speaks in

Matthew 7 could have come to that very conclusion in their lifetimes. I can imagine them standing before Jesus, stunned, and thinking to themselves, "Whoa! Doesn't the Bible say we are not saved by faith alone, but that works are needed to make our faith alive?* Something's wrong! We told Jesus He was our Lord. We did the works that He told us to do. And we did them *in His name*! Now He's saying we're workers of iniquity! He's saying only those who do the will of God will get into Heaven! Weren't we doing the will of God?"

They thought they had faith, and they thought they had works, but something was missing.

Could there be a third aspect to faith – besides believing God's Word and acting on it – without which faith is useless or non-genuine?

Now that we have a foundation for gaining truth, it seems a good time to speak of essential elements, which will lead us to the point of this book – i.e., what a three-legged stool has to do with faith.

---

*Some believe they are saved by faith. But in truth, the Bible does not say we are saved by faith. It says we are saved by God's grace *through* faith. (Ephesians 2:8) That may seem a small distinction to some, especially those who speak of "saving faith," but actually, the distinction is huge. If salvation came by our decision, our works, our efforts, then it would not be a gift of God. Do we have to make the decision? Yes, but it is no more our works than the acceptance of an invitation to a party makes the party our work.

CHAPTER THREE

Without Which, Nothing
(Essential Elements)

A man owned a beautiful automobile, which sat in his driveway day and night for all to see. He loved cleaning and polishing the car. It was so stunning it gave him a sense of status, of achievement. Some of his neighbors wondered why he never drove it, assuming he was a bit eccentric. No one knew until one night when a young man, overcome by the desire to have the car, tried to steal it. He failed because, to his astonishment, the beautiful car had no engine. It was useless for driving, because it was just a shell that served its owner for appearances only.

An essential element was missing that would make the car useful.

The Latin phrase, *sine qua non*, is an interesting phrase. Literally translated, it means *without which not*, or *without which nothing*. The phrase is used to describe absolutely indispensable things. You could say that faith is a *sine qua non* of Christianity, because without faith, it is impossible to please God. (Hebrews 11:6)

We could say that sunlight is a *sine qua non* for life on earth. It is not the only indispensable element. There are many indispensables to life on earth: air, water, clouds, the presence of nourishing edibles, gravity and so on.

Biochemist Michael Behe coined the term "irreducible complexity" to describe biological systems whose elements are so integral to the successful functioning of the system that evolutionary theory cannot account for their appearance in a species. That is, all of the necessary parts would have to appear and be functional simultaneously in order to make the system a survival enhancement instead of a survival handicap. The "irreducible" aspect means that if any element were removed, the system would no longer be functional and, therefore, the system itself would no longer contribute to survival of the species.

All of God's physical creation shows evidence of intelligent design, often with essential elements in delicate balance. Things so diverse as the human body, hen eggs, heavy metals, crystals, bird wings, and even a tiny drop of water, are masterpieces of design. So much so that, if we did not know that the eyes of the unsaved are blinded by the enemy of our souls, it would be incredible that any educated person would actually believe that such things are the result of chance (evolution). One might even say that creation exhibits a vast "knowledge" of physics and engineering, even though these concepts merely reflect man's discovery of what God demonstrated in nature.

For the purposes of this book, let's say that design is the idea that various elements may be positioned in such a way as to work together to form a cohesive unit. When the elements work so well together that each is integral to the successful formation of the end product, and no needed elements are missing, the cohesive unit may be said to have integrity. Removal of any element in such a design negates its integrity; that is, it changes the end product so dramatically that it is no longer what it previously was or no longer has the potential it previously had.

For example, fire requires three elements: fuel, oxygen and heat sufficient for combustion. Each component is integral to the mixture, so that without either one, fire cannot exist. It must have all three; they form a triad that, in the proper proportions, becomes fire. Remove either element and you cannot start a fire.

Life shows us many combinations in delicate balance, things made up of essential parts with no unnecessary ingredients. Even elements we consider basic to life, such as air and water, are combinations of molecules in wonderful balance. Remove the oxygen atom from an H_2O molecule and the result is no longer water, but hydrogen. Add a second oxygen atom and the result is hydrogen peroxide. The air we breathe contains oxygen, nitrogen, argon and trace elements of carbon dioxide. A relatively slight shift in the balance of elements in our atmosphere could create radical changes in life on Earth.

Why would we think that only physical elements possess design? You are a design, for example, a melding of the physical with the intangible – spirit, soul and body.

In Genesis 1:26, God said, *"Let us make man in our image..."*

Just as He is a three-part Being – Father, Son and Holy Spirit – we are three-part beings, made up of spirit, soul and body. And just as the Father, Son and Holy Spirit are in agreement, to the extent of being One, God expects us, corporately and as individuals, to be united by agreement in spirit, soul and body.

The apostle Paul wrote, *"And the very God of peace sanctify you wholly; and I pray God your whole spirit and soul and body be preserved blameless unto the coming of our Lord Jesus Christ."* I Thessalonians 5:23

You are actually the innermost one of your three integral parts, a spirit possessing a soul (consisting of a mind, will and emotions) and inhabiting a body – notwithstanding the fact that, until you are born again, your spirit self is "dead" to God. Nevertheless, if somehow one of the three elements is removed, you can readily see that you will no longer be what you previously were.

I believe you will soon see that such an intangible thing as faith is also the result of God's design. And as such, it is possibly the most misunderstood concept of all time. In America, we think of faith as "belief," which, alone, is a pretty vague concept in the understanding of many people just learning English. Why? Because "belief" can have a range of meanings in the English language, from the shallowest form of understanding to the deepest form of trust.

To demonstrate, here are some examples.

"I believe I left my car keys on the dresser."

"Do you believe in love at first sight?"

"I believe Frankfort is the capital of Kentucky."

"I'm a believer in taking vitamins."

Compare these uses of the idea with, *"Believe on the Lord Jesus Christ and you shall be saved, and your house."*

Do the former bear close resemblance to the latter? No. It would be extreme to imagine the former kinds of belief having any significant impact on one's life comparable to the belief spoken of in Acts 16:31. The latter form of belief is the basis on which we must hang all of eternity.

Therefore, we cannot rely on the meanings that exist in men's minds. We must discern and operate according to the meaning that God intends, as revealed in the body of His Word, the Bible. Scriptural faith, as it exists in the mind of God, is made up of parts that are absolutely essential to the integrity of the concept. Remove either from the equation and the result is no longer scriptural faith.

A stool might conceivably have many legs, but if it is to function, it must have at least three. Three legs is the irreducible number for lateral stability, and the minimum essential to keep it free-standing. The complementary "legs" brace and buttress each other against opposing forces. Each transfers strength and energy to the others. You will soon see how that analogy applies to faith.

The most important aspect of the three-legged stool, for the purposes of this book, is that each leg is absolutely essential to the integrity of the stool. Remove either leg and the stool can no longer stand alone. In fact, it will no longer meet the definition of a stool. Rather, it is relegated to a very shaky support, which is exactly the way we must view any kind of faith that does not meet the three-legged test of faith.

Now let's look at these essential ingredients and examine why they are vital to genuine faith.

CHAPTER FOUR

Belief versus *True* Belief

The communication model popularized by Canadian educator Marshall McLuhan in the 1960s assumes three parts to any exchange of ideas: a "sender," a "receiver" and a message. Without either element, communication does not occur.

Elementary to the communication of faith is an assumption of three factors: a person who possesses faith, the one true God as the object of faith and the truth believed about God, i.e., what He has said and done.

Paul said in Romans 10:17, *"faith cometh by hearing, and hearing by the word of God."* That means the only source of true faith is God's Word. Not the Qur'an. Not the Bhagavad Gita. Not in The Watchtower Society writings. Not in the Book of Mormon, the Buddhists' Tipitaka, Taoist texts, Dianetics, Divine Principle, astrology, folklore, wives' tales, tradition, fantasy, other "spiritual" writings, things people imagine and what they merely hope is true – neither is a valid source of faith. Faith can only be obtained from the Holy Bible.

You may think of yourself as a person of faith, but if your faith is not invested in the right object – the one true God – and is not based on what He has led His prophets to record in the Bible, your faith is not genuine. Always remember this fundamental truth about genuine faith: it comes only by the Word of God, the Holy Bible.

Not only does faith come only from God's Word, it comes by an earnest consideration of the *entire* Word of God, not fragments. (No, that doesn't mean you have to know and understand the entire Bible before you can have faith. You must have a heart that does not pick and choose what to believe in His Word.) Some people skip the "hard parts" in the Bible but still give themselves credit for treasuring God's Word. We cannot have a "holey" Bible, with gaping voids of passages we either do not believe or do not even consider because they do not fit with our current beliefs. We subject ourselves to serious error by placing doctrinal boundaries inside God's Word, refusing to hear what the Holy Spirit has to say about aspects of the Bible that we have ignored or have been told are not important.

We must be open to and seek God for the entire truth. When we reject or discount any part of His Word for any reason, we are saying to God that we are capable of deciding how much of Him and His truth we should know.

We have all heard the story of three men, blindfolded, who each touched different parts of an elephant and attempted to describe what he was touching. The one who touched a leg thought it was a tree. The one who touched the tail imagined he was gripping a cable. The man who felt the trunk believed it to be a fire hose. They formed their beliefs from a limited perspective.

John 3:16 is certainly the most popular and the most quoted verse in the New Testament, perhaps in the entire Bible. But when it comes to salvation, it is virtually the only verse some people know about the subject, and consequently it contains the sum of their understanding of it: i.e., Belief in Jesus Christ equals salvation.

"For God so loved the world that he gave his only begotten Son, that whosoever believeth in him should not perish, but have everlasting life."

I am not suggesting that this scripture is not true, because it is. What I am here to tell you is that the word "believe" does not mean what some might think it means.

There is a kind of belief that requires no investment of self in order to acquire. It is the kind of belief that believes tomorrow is Tuesday or that the shade of green one is examining is called chartreuse. It is *simple belief.* Being wrong about simple belief does not usually result in dire consequences.

In America, belief is not a requirement for obeying the laws of the land. You must obey the laws whether you *believe* they are right and good or senseless. The United States justice system requires of citizens certain actions, and the requirement to act according to the law supersedes belief in or justification of those laws. (From the legal perspective, that is. From God's perspective, of course, His Word supersedes secular laws when they oppose His Word.)

Likewise, there is no law against beliefs in America, as of this writing at least. There are restrictions against *acting* upon certain beliefs, of course, but for now, beliefs themselves are untouchable. What one does or does not believe is of little consequence in the secular world. You may change, refute, contradict, misstate, affirm, deny or forget your beliefs altogether and your life will be virtually unaffected from a secular standpoint. Some politicians regularly prove this to be true.

Neither simple belief nor lack of it has any lasting consequence, except perhaps your belief about who has the right-of-way at a traffic signal, or whether you can fly when diving off a building. Even in an educational setting, belief is not required to pass exams. For example, believing that George Washington was the first president of the United States is not a requirement of any history course. You might need to state that he was the first U.S. president in order to score a correct answer on a quiz, but you are not required to believe it is true.

However, belief, in the Biblical context, is a complex concept. Let me clarify. It is complex in that it has more than a single component, but it is not complex in terms of difficulty to understand.

When Jesus spoke of belief, He communicated something altogether different than what twenty-first century Americans think of as belief. The Greek word *pisteuo* (pist-yoo'-o), which is translated "believes" in John 3:16, means "to have faith in or upon; to entrust, believe or commit to; or to put in trust with."

While an examination of that Greek word hints at its depth of meaning, the truth of it is revealed only when the whole context is sought.

Here's an example why context is so important. The final verse in chapter three of the gospel of John says the following in the King James translation of the Bible:

"He that believeth on the Son hath everlasting life: and he that believeth not the Son shall not see life; but the wrath of God abideth on him." V. 36 (Emphasis added)

The statement seems to be one of simple comparison: believing versus not believing. However, a look at the Greek reveals a distinction not seen in the KJV. Just as in John 3:16, *pisteuo* is the Greek word translated as "believeth" in the first part of the sentence. In the second instance, however, "believeth not" comes from the Greek word *apeitheo*, which means to disbelieve willfully and disobey, and in the American Standard translation, is rendered "obeys not." *Apeitheo* is also used in the KJV, in Romans 2:8, when referring to those who "do not obey" the truth.

A moment of logic is in order here. Writers of the New Testament used Greek to communicate the teachings of Jesus. They used a language very common in the geographic area in which they lived. They could have used Hebrew or any number of languages, but Greek was what they used. Any human language is very limited, you must admit, when trying to communicate to the human heart what is in the mind of God. Therefore students of the Bible cannot single out any one scripture – such as John 3:16 – or lean on a superficial reading of scripture for a correct, comprehensive understanding of God's message.

When God speaks to His children, He can communicate volumes in nanoseconds without an audible word. It is then the task of the hearer, or recipient, to put the communication into human verbiage, if that is necessary. After all, before man came onto the scene in the Garden of Eden, God needed no language whatsoever to communicate to angels. Human language is largely inadequate for understanding God's missives, and can at times be a stumbling block to true understanding. Language can only attempt to communicate the understanding received from the Holy Spirit. Understanding the communication of the Holy Spirit is the job of the heart.

Not only can human language be a stumbling block, but so can human motivation. Without a love for the truth and a willingness to be conformed to it, rather than to conform the truth to one's own preconceived notions, no one can extract the truth from the Word of God. I have encountered people who considered themselves satisfactory Bible scholars because they read through the Bible once. I've talked with drunks who used their superficial reading of God's Word – "Jesus drank wine!" they have said – to rationalize their daily over-consumption of alcohol. It is common knowledge that many cults take only certain passages of the scriptures – omitting huge inconvenient passages – to justify their aberrant beliefs and allow themselves to maintain control of their own lives.

In short, beliefs are transitory unless one seeks the truth and insists on having nothing but the truth. A man or woman who does not believe that God exists does not believe His truth exists, and will therefore fall for anything. Even with a belief in God, a man or woman who will not sacrifice his or her own limited concept of truth in order to obtain God's truth is doomed. To love one's own thoughts and preconceived notions is a dangerous undertaking, for it can lead to rejection of anything that does not agree with them.

The Bible is a large body of writing, and is far deeper than its words. It is so big, you cannot hold on to any singled-out portion of it blindfolded, as it were, or "looking through a glass darkly," and expect that it will give you a grasp of the whole body. Many people have gone astray by accepting the words of men who claim their understanding of the Bible – whether denominational doctrine or personal belief – is the authoritative interpretation.

Only the Holy Spirit can guide you to understanding. And He only gives it personally, individually. Heart to heart.

There's one more thing you need to understand about gaining the truth from the Word of God, and this may be the hardest to swallow for some.

God has hidden His deep truths. And some will never find them.

Paul told the Corinthians, *"But we speak the wisdom of God in a mystery, even the hidden wisdom, which God ordained before the world unto our glory:"* (1Corinthians 2:7) Just as God hid the Garden of Eden from Adam and Eve and all of mankind (Genesis 3:24) after man sinned, He hid much of His truth from fallen man until the time when He chose to reveal it through the Holy Spirit.

Paul continued by saying, *"Eye hath not seen, nor ear heard, neither have entered into the heart of man, the things which God hath prepared for them that love him. But God hath revealed them unto us by his Spirit: for the Spirit searcheth all things, yea, the deep things of God."* (vv. 9-10) The coming of the Holy Spirit opened the way for us to freely receive the true riches of God.

Perhaps in your lifetime you have found the Word of God hard to understand. Has it ever occurred to you that God could have made it a lot simpler to understand? Of course He could, but He purposely made it difficult to understand.

What? God would hide truth from people even though knowing the truth could save them? Isn't the Word of God so simple that even a child can understand it?

You will have to hear this from Jesus's own mouth before you can begin to understand.

Jesus had just given a sermon we call the "parable of the sower," and the multitude that had been gathered to Him left. They may have left in the same manner that we often see people leaving a church building on Sundays, as they shake hands with the pastor and say, "Good message, preacher," but they walk away without having their lives changed.

On this occasion, in Mark 4, some of Jesus's disciples along with the twelve chosen followers remained behind. Listen to the amazing truth Jesus reveals about the purposely hidden mysteries of God.

"And he said unto them, He that hath ears to hear, let him hear. And when he was alone, they that were about him with the twelve asked of him the parable. And he said unto them, Unto you it is given to know the mystery of the kingdom of God: but unto them that are without, all these things are done in parables: That seeing they may see, and not perceive; and hearing they may hear, and not

understand; lest at any time they should be converted, and their sins should be forgiven them." Mark 4: 9-12

Did you get that? The disciples wanted to know what His sermon *meant*. They did not just listen to the message and immediately walk away to tend to their own business like many among the multitude did. They knew Jesus was giving them something of great value, even though they did not understand what He was saying. They valued His words enough to seek out the deeper truth, to learn how to apply it to their lives. They loved and desired truth. And because they did, Jesus declared they would be given the opportunity to know the "mystery" of the kingdom of God.

(AUTHOR'S NOTE: See 2 Thessalonians 2:10 again to understand how important it is to love truth.)

Now notice what Jesus said about the multitude who walked away without asking for the meaning. He said they were "without" and that they were the reason He spoke in parables, *"That seeing they may see, and not perceive; and hearing they may hear, and not understand."* Without what? Without ears to hear (v.9). He did not intend to make God's truth clear to those whose hearts were not prepared to hear it, and who did not value it enough to dig deeper for its meaning and application to their lives.

Some hear the Word of God preached, but they have their spiritual eyes "glazed over," in a zombie-like stupor, not truly hungering for it. They let their minds wander, dwelling on distractions of a temporal nature rather than dwelling on the truth God has sent to set them free. Simply hearing the Word of God does not mean we mix it with faith. The writer of Hebrews said, *"For indeed we have had glad tidings presented to us, even as they also; but the word of the report did not profit them, not being mixed with faith in those who heard."* (Hebrew 4:2) Faith does come by hearing the Word of God, as Romans 10:17 says, but we have to do the mixing – i.e., the mixing of our faith with God's truth.

And here was Jesus's reason for not making God's hidden truths clear to those who were without: *"lest at any time they should be converted, and their sins should be forgiven them."* He was saying that if He made things too plain, those who were "without" might become converted! The Greek word *exo*, translated here as "without" can also be translated as "outside," "away," "out of," or even "strange." Because they did not have ears to hear, they were strangers to the truth.

Does that sound at all like the God your Sunday School teacher told you about? In Sunday School, many are told that Jesus spoke in parables so that everyone, including children, could understand. But that is not in the Bible. The reason children can often understand deep truths of God's Word is not because the truths are made clear through parables. They understand them because their own hearts are uncomplicated and uncluttered, eager to believe, unlike like those of many adults.

No, God hid the beautiful truths of His Word from those who *did not* have the unprejudiced, unencumbered hearts of children. He hid it from those who did not value it, did not love it, as evidenced by the fact that they did not seek its inner beauty and truth to change their lives.

Many tradition-oriented Christians will reject the idea that God has hidden His truth from some, but Jesus compared the riches of God's truths to a hidden treasure. *"Again, the kingdom of heaven is like unto treasure hid in a field; the which when a man hath found, he hideth, and for joy thereof goeth and selleth all that he hath, and buyeth that field."* Matthew 13:44

God expects us to value His Word above everything, to sacrifice anything that stands in the way of having it. (If you just had the thought, "No, He expects us to value Jesus above all else," please recall that Jesus is the Word of God made flesh. John 1:1, 14)

How many times have you heard the Bible preached or taught *without* going to the Word of God yourself to read and to ask the Holy Spirit to explain what you heard?

Ask yourself, "Do I love the Word of God? Do I love its truth and beauty enough to search it out and ask the

Holy Spirit to give me understanding? Do I really trust the Holy Spirit to be my personal Teacher?"

If you don't, then ask God for a greater love for His Word.

You and I must love the Word of God enough to dig into it.

The Psalmist said, *"The secret of the LORD is with them that fear him; and he will shew them his covenant."* (Psalm 25:14) God made a mystery of His Word, hiding great, valuable truths as secrets from superficial listeners. Paul told the Corinthians:

"But we speak the wisdom of God in a mystery, even the hidden wisdom, which God ordained before the world unto our glory:...But as it is written, Eye hath not seen, nor ear heard, neither have entered into the heart of man, the things which God hath prepared for them that love him. But God hath revealed them unto us by his Spirit: for the Spirit searcheth all things, yea, the deep things of God." (I Corinthians 2:7, 9-10)

Most of us hide valuables to keep them safe. You hide your treasured possessions from those who think they can become wealthy with little effort, by stealing from you and others that which is valuable. You don't hide treasures from those you can trust, but only from those who don't value them in the same way you do. Sure, thieves value your treasures, but only as something to be obtained quickly, cheaply and with as little effort or investment of themselves as possible.

If someone truly values a pearl of great price, he will sell all he has to own it; he will not subsequently toss it before swine, to have it trampled on.

God's truth will not be purchased with simple belief, or with belief – to paraphrase King David – that costs the hearer nothing. It will be obtained by a more meaningful belief, one that involves an exchange by one's self.

We must value what He values in order to find what He has hidden for us. Thus, some will never find His treasures.

Beware if you do not love God's Word enough to seek its hidden treasures! Do not be satisfied with the sermons you hear. Do not assume you have what you need when you receive it second-hand, as it were, from a minister or some other intermediary between you and God Himself. The death and resurrection of Jesus Christ made the way for us to have the great privilege of being taught by the Holy Spirit Himself. Do not count that as something insignificant.

In this world are treasures of gold, silver, jewels and, of course, greenbacks. But in the kingdom of God, these are what some might call "chump change." In Luke 16, verses 10 and 11, Jesus refers to "unrighteous mammon," or worldly wealth, as that which is least. Perhaps that's why He makes the worldly riches available to all. They're not so valuable to Him that they must be hidden from mankind. He provides mammon (money) to see how we'll use small things. He makes "the true riches" available to those who show themselves faithful as stewards over the least of His blessings, continuing to serve Him instead of mammon – and even submitting mammon to His purposes.

In other words, when we refuse to serve money, choosing instead to serve God and to cause money to serve God, He can trust us with the truly valuable treasures of life that come only through knowing Him and His Word. Treasures such as wisdom, joy, love, peace – all the fruit of the Holy Spirit and the character of God – as well as truth. These are part of the treasures He hides from those who are "outside." They can only come to those who know and love God (through Jesus Christ) and who treasure what He treasures.

By faith, we may obtain God's hidden riches. The Lord gives us an "allowance" of faith, much the way a man will pour a small amount of water into a hand pump to "prime" it. In fact, Romans 12: 3 says, "...*God hath dealt to every man the measure of faith*." That measure is enough for us to begin the discovery of His treasures, but sadly, many bury that initial gift of a measure and never begin the search for greater understanding.

He wants us to use our faith, to increase it, to take little faith and make it great faith. I have been told that the parable of the talents deals with money and with special gifts and natural abilities that we have come to call "talents." I do not dispute that. But because the Word of God teaches principles and fundamental truths as well as specific truths for specific instances, I also believe that the parable applies to the measure of faith. God expects a return on the faith He gives us. As we use our faith for His glory in the earth, not only does it do exactly that – bring Him glory – but it also increases itself in us. If we bury our measure of faith in the ground, we will be held to account for our failure to bring Him a return on His investment.*

Faith is made to be put into action, to be used for God's kingdom.

From God's perspective, belief is inseparable from corresponding action. Only hypocrites say they believe something and then act in a manner that belies their statement. So it turns out that Biblical belief also requires works, or proof. If faith is passive, it is not genuine faith.

"They profess that they know God; but in works they deny Him." Titus 1:16

And...

"Yea, a man may say, Thou hast faith, and I have works: shew me thy faith without thy works, and I will shew thee my faith by my works." James 2:18

Therefore, while the secular system of laws requires actions foremost, regardless of belief, God's system requires belief that results in or expresses itself in corresponding action. Works alone do not bring us to righteousness.

"For if Abraham were justified by works, he hath whereof to glory; but not before God. For what saith the scripture? Abraham believed God, and it was counted unto him for righteousness. Now to him that worketh is the reward not reckoned of grace, but of debt. But to him that worketh not, but believeth on him that justifieth the ungodly, his faith is counted for righteousness." Romans 4:2-5

Again, the Bible says we are saved by grace. Yet works are necessary.

Lest I confuse you, let's use the next chapter to look a little deeper at the age-old conflict between faith and works.

*NOTE: Some may try to draw an analogy between God's tactic of hiding wisdom and truth from those who are without and the actions of the "wicked and lazy servant" (Mathew 25:14-26) with one talent who hid it in the ground. But these two are far removed. God gave every man the key with which to unlock the mysteries of God. That key was faith in Him and His Word. Some will never use that key. God hid the treasures, but not the key to finding the treasures. If a man hides that key, not putting its value to use for himself and for God, but seeing it as an object with mysterious meaning, of value to the Giver only, that man has counted the key and the treasures as worthless.

CHAPTER FIVE

Faith Versus Works

Throughout the ages, religious people have debated the value of works relative to faith. The one side has declared that faith requires nothing more than belief, because grace paid the entire price for sin. The other side has stood on works alone for justification before God.

Either side is able to find scriptures that seem to support its belief. For example, Romans 3:28 (see below) seems to support the idea that works are unnecessary, while James 2:18 seems to support the primacy of works over faith.

"Therefore we conclude that a man is justified by faith without the deeds of the law." Romans 3:28

"...I will shew thee my faith by my works." James 2:18

Theologians have observed of certain cults, such as Jehovah's Witnesses, that they are trying to work their way into God's favor. They knock on doors and hand out literature because they are told that works are of primary importance in having a place in God's kingdom. Likewise, it is said of the Mormons that they, too, are trying to earn their way into heaven in part by physical reproduction, because some believe the more babies they produce, the more like God they become.

My purpose here is not to distinguish between cults and their beliefs, or to identify their errors, but to point out what it means to put your trust in works. The scriptural fact is, people who place their trust in their own efforts as their primary entrée to God are attempting to circumvent grace. They have manufactured a "righteousness" that does not rely solely on the righteousness of Jesus Christ.

"Now to him that worketh is the reward not reckoned of grace, but of debt." Romans 4:4

Let it be abundantly clear that none of us can perform enough works to circumvent God's grace made available in Christ, for it is by the grace of God that we even have the disposition to believe in Jesus Christ. When Peter correctly identified Jesus as "the Christ, the Son of the Living God," Jesus declared, *"Blessed art thou, Simon Barjona: for flesh and blood hath not revealed it unto thee, but My Father which is in heaven."* (Matthew 16:17-18)

As it was true with Peter, it is true with us – we owe even our belief in Jesus Christ to the revelatory grace of God.

(AUTHOR'S NOTE: Some people bristle at the use of the word revelation in the context of Christians hearing from God. The intent here, in speaking of "revelatory grace," is that the truth of what God revealed in His Word be fully revealed to us.)

Trusting works to earn salvation is the kind of backward relationship between faith and works that prompted Paul to say to the Galatians,

"O foolish Galatians, who hath bewitched you, that ye should not obey the truth, before whose eyes Jesus Christ hath been evidently set forth, crucified among you?" Galatians 3:1

Grace gives us the entrance, through faith, into salvation that it was not possible for works to give. Grace opens the way for us to trust in Jesus. If grace would save us without faith, then any belief or lifestyle would be satisfactory for entrance into God's presence. However, grace makes the way open, faith shows the way (Jesus Christ) that is open, and works are the actions we take as we walk in that way. Grace neither eliminates the need for faith and works, nor provides a license to walk in any other direction. What grace does do, however, is *enable* works of faith. Paul said it was the grace of God that produced labor through him.

"But by the grace of God I am what I am: and his grace which was bestowed upon me was not in vain; but I labored more abundantly than they all: yet not I, but the grace of God which was with me." I Corinthians 15:10

The place of works is in following grace and faith, not to supplant either. We labor through grace – unless grace was bestowed upon us in vain.

In truth, works are an inseparable ingredient of faith, for James has said that faith without works is dead. There is a faith that does not produce works. However, that is not the kind of faith God supplies and expects to receive from us in return.

That's right, He *supplies* faith. It comes from His word, as we are told in Romans 10. He gives us faith, and we return it to Him. So when Jesus speaks of believing, we cannot understand the word He used any other way than with the assumption that it is the kind of faith that produces works.

"For by grace are ye saved through faith; and that not of yourselves: it is the gift of God: Not of works, lest any man should boast. For we are his workmanship, created in Christ Jesus unto good works, which God hath before ordained that we should walk in them." Ephesians 2:8-10

We have been created in Christ Jesus unto good works. Works are what we do after we have received salvation through grace, not to earn salvation.

Faith and works, then, follow a sequence. To use a cliché, we cannot put the cart before the horse. Think of faith as the horse, works as the cart and grace as the path on which the horse pulls the cart. With the horse of faith pulling, leading in the right direction, the cart of works follows. If the horse tries to push the cart, it will inevitably veer off the path. To speak more plainly, if genuine faith leads on the path of grace, then works must follow. However, if works lead, then faith will certainly veer away from grace. Jesus also indicated as much in Mark 16:17, when He said that *"signs will follow those that believe."*

We do not follow signs; they are supposed to follow us because we believe.

To confirm this order, remember the promise of God to Abraham, that He would make him the father of many nations. Abraham believed God. He trusted God's promise to him, and waited patiently for it to become manifest – *25 years later.* (See Genesis 12:2-4 & 21:1-5) Now, when Abraham believed and obeyed, faith was opened to the entire Jewish nation that was to come. That happened because God made a promise. He gave His Word to Abraham. However, 430 years later, God instituted the law by Moses because the Israelites were not being obedient to the faith. The law came to force God's people to be obedient because they could not do so on their own. Read Galatians 3:16-18 to see how Paul shows this preeminence of faith (in God's promise) over works that are acts of obedience to the faith.

The truth is: obedience is always in response to a command or to knowledge of the wishes of the one who commands. No knowledge of a command or commander, no obedience. Works done in response to one's own decisions or desires are dead works; works done in response to God's Word have the power to be good works when they come from a desire to please Him.

"*Without faith it is impossible to please God,*" says the writer of Hebrews. So we know we cannot discount faith, expecting works alone to save us. Works without faith produces self-righteousness, or at best, self-righteous philanthropy.

But so-called faith without corresponding actions is hypocrisy. It is dead faith. That's why God said of unbelieving Israel, "*...these people draw near to Me with their mouths and honor Me with their lips, but have removed their hearts far from Me...*" (Isaiah 29:13) Therefore, faith alone is unacceptable.

We are told that salvation is free. Some may suggest that if it is truly free, then it does not require works. But the truth is that while it is free it does require an exchange. A giving up of the old and a wholehearted embracing of the new.

Are those two conditions – free, but requiring an exchange – incompatible? Not at all. Here's an example.

Suppose you have driven an old truck so long it has fallen apart. Although it has been cantankerous and unreliable, you are at least comfortable with it. But fraught with mechanical problems, eaten through by rust, a pain in your back when you have had to drive it farther than a few miles, the old beast has finally given up its frail hold on usefulness, and has died.

Then suppose your father sees your struggle, knowing that you don't have the means of repairing it or the money to replace it. One day, when he sees you go out and get into the rusting heap to just sit, he realizes your sentimentality over the old truck is neither productive nor healthy. He feels so bad for you that he decides to buy you a brand new truck. And he gives it to you, free. No strings attached *except* that you give up the old one.

It is a gift. What is the logical thing you should do? Would you reject the new truck and keep the old one for the sake of sentimentality, or get rid of the old truck and drive the new one?

Most people would have the old truck hauled away and gladly drive the new one. They would gladly exchange the old for the new. The old truck would not amount to a trade-in or even a down payment. In fact, it is barely an exchange at all, given the useless and even dangerous condition of what is being relinquished, compared to the great value of the thing received.

You could not be said to fully value and appreciate the free gift of a new truck if you continued to pine over and long for the crankiness – or possibly the "non-crankiness" – of the old truck. Likewise, you cannot be considered to fully receive and appreciate the new life in Christ if you still hold on to the old life, continuing to try making it run right using the old ways.

No, God wants us to make a thorough exchange. We are to fully give up our old, dead lives and fruitless ways of thinking and acting when we accept the free gift of His new, eternal life in Christ. We have no need of two when one is fully adequate and the other is counter-productive.

A man who refused the free gift of a brand new truck in order to try to resurrect a dead and useless truck would be viewed with a good deal of astonishment by most people. Yet many who hear the gospel, who ask for the free gift of salvation and call themselves followers of Christ, have not given up the old life. Listening to the same faithless, secular music, being entertained by the same crude ideas and images, thinking and acting out the same sinful patterns of life, they are like the man with the old truck, wanting to keep the old rusting carcasses of their former lives around, pining over their loss of the thing with which they have identified for so long, and continuing to go out in the driveway to sit in the truck, wishing it would somehow revive and bring back their old times.

That kind of attitude in a Christian is symptomatic of a complete misunderstanding of the exchange required, and of the relative values of the old life versus the new.

Someone who has not made the exchange fully may never have made the exchange at all. True faith in

Christ must produce actions in concert with His Word.

The only conclusion to draw is that faith in the absence of corresponding works is not the scriptural kind of believing. Genuine faith is the kind of faith that produces works. One without the other is incomplete. No lesser definition for "belief" can withstand scriptural scrutiny.

Yet if we stop here, we are lost.

Why? Because we saw people in Matthew chapter seven who called Jesus "Lord," who believed so strongly that they did scriptural works in His name, and yet, who were rejected by Jesus.

If we are willing to look a bit further into scripture, we will find that scriptural believing contains yet another essential ingredient.

CHAPTER SIX

Faith *With* Works...Alive or Dead?

Who among us has not had an idea for an appliance at some time or other that, if perfected, could make life easier or more enjoyable for people? What has stopped us? Probably most of us were stymied by how to actually make the thing work successfully and reliably. Ideas are great. But they are useless in the absence of a proper "how to" plan for completion.

In any working construct, there is an idea or concept of an end product that is to be achieved. Then there must be a mechanism or means by which the result is achieved. And, of course, there is the motivating or powering force, if you will, that puts the mechanism in motion to produce the desired end. As an example, let's look at a simple ice cream churn.

The inventor of the ice cream churn desired for the ice-cream-making process to be easy and produce a consistently smooth product. That was the concept. The means or mechanism was a rotating paddle inside a consistently turning can, into which the proper ingredients were to be held in a freezing-cold environment (ice). The motivating force or motion-producing energy was a person's own energy and strength applied to a crank.

One day, someone had the idea of using electricity as the motivating force to drive the mechanism. That change made a tremendous difference in producing ice cream at home.

Now the application, spiritually, is this: God desires that someone accomplish a specific objective in His will, meaning, His Word. That is the concept, or the idea He conceived. The means of accomplishing it is some form of action that we respond with, say, in giving of our time, energy and/or material goods.

Those two elements – the concept and the means – are inadequate without some sort of motivation. Many good intentions fall flat for lack of motivation. People are motivated in many ways, including by fear, a desire to exalt one's self, to repay an obligation, a sense of guilt, a desire for reward, or for love. You might be able to think of others.

However, God desires that we operate by a specific motivating force to initiate and complete the process of accomplishing His will.

The word "motive" comes from the Latin word, *motus*, which means "to move." The dictionary definition of motive is "something that causes a person to act."

We could try to obey God by the motive of obligation and produce apparent obedience. The same is true of the motivations of fear, a desire for self-glorification, the expectation of a superficial reward or any number of motives. But to Him, the only motive that truly pleases is the primary one that motivates Him: love.

Therefore the entire construct of obedience is only complete, in His view, when the motive pleases Him.

Following Jesus is not a lip-service adherence to a doctrinal position coupled with a superficial obedience to a few scriptural commands.

The psalmist said:

"Who shall ascend into the hill of the LORD? or who shall stand in his holy place? He that hath clean hands, and a pure heart; who hath not lifted up his soul unto vanity, nor sworn deceitfully." Psalms 24:3-4

This Psalm speaks of a person who is fully committed to having the character of Christ in his heart. If we have not lived up to this kind of obedience, we must repent and ask God to correct us and help us to walk with "clean hands and a pure heart."

Consider a child who will do what you tell him to do, but without being fully committed to loving you as his motive. The child might comply with what you instruct him to do, but his heart is not in it. Thus, the "obedience" is not perfect obedience, since the heart motive is left out of the equation. A parent who settles for a child's legal compliance without his heart-felt willingness to obey through love for the parent is not doing the child any favors. Such a child could learn to bypass love altogether, even though love is the very heart of the parent-child relationship. Paul wrote that *"the letter* [of the law] *killeth, but the spirit giveth life."* 2 Corinthians 3:6

No, children must be taught, through demonstration, what it means to obey out of love.

Likewise, love is the very heart of our relationship with God, love that is mutually expressive and tender. Jesus asked God if there could be any way around the cross, but quickly added, *"Nevertheless, not my will, but thine be done."* (Luke 22:42)

I have seen children rebel, refusing to obey, and I have seen them resentfully comply. As a parent, I conclude that neither is the kind of response a parent truly wants, and neither is the kind of obedience our Father wants of us. Given our own preference, we might not want to do a certain thing that God instructs us to do, but if we will subjugate our will to His in loving submission to and agreement with Him, desiring to please Him with our actions, and obey Him, we will be exercising the kind of obedience that does indeed please Him.

Now, I would like to briefly address the question of holiness. Some people have the belief that holiness is a strict obedience to the word of God. They may or may not be of the congregations that require their members to abstain from outward forms of worldliness in clothing and entertainment. Holiness is certainly a requirement of God, and we must have works that are evident in our lifestyles and clothing, at least to the extent that we do not dress or act in a way that might cause another to stumble. But there is a kind of so-called holiness that men adopt that equates works alone, even after salvation, with the holiness God expects of us. That is not true holiness.

Just as a child may comply with a parent's wishes in the total absence of any joy and desire in doing so, believers also may adopt an attitude toward obedience that has neither true joy in the act nor any love in its motive. Again, this kind of diligence may seem admirable, as it reflects obedience with "mind, soul and strength," with which we are to love God, but lacks the involvement of the heart, which God included in the equation. (Mark 12:30)

When scripture says that *"God loves a cheerful giver"* (2 Corinthians 9:7), it is entirely plausible this is not just true of giving money. I believe God loves cheerfulness in all forms of giving, including of our time, energy and sacrifices.

It might be easy to miss the importance of love in the scheme of faith. It is apparent that the church knows we're *supposed* to love each other. But the way we practice that love makes it appear we think love is an option instead of the only commandment which we have been given in Christ.

Given the sad condition of the church in America today, our actions as a whole suggest we think that as long as we "believe in Jesus," we will be welcomed into heaven. However, I don't think the church at large, at least in America, has seen how integral love is to our salvation. It is so integral to faith and works that neither is genuine without it.

Love is the core of Christianity. Indeed, we are assured that if we obey the command to love God with all our hearts, minds, souls and strength, and love our neighbors as ourselves, we will satisfy all other commandments. A person who loves God will do everything possible not to sin against Him. A person who loves his neighbor as himself will do everything possible not to sin against him, and moreover, will do whatever he can to see that person depart from sin, to enter the kingdom of God and to have all the blessings of God wherewith he has himself been blessed.

According to Paul, heart motivation is the element that makes the bond between faith and works genuine. If you read I Corinthians 13, you quickly find that NEITHER FAITH NOR WORKS amounts to anything if LOVE is not at the heart of it.

"Though I speak with the tongues of men and of angels, and have not charity, I am become as sounding brass, or a tinkling cymbal. And though I have the gift of prophecy, and understand all mysteries, and all knowledge; and though I have all faith, so that I could remove mountains, and have not charity, I am nothing. And though I bestow all my goods to feed the poor, and though I give my body to be burned, and have not charity, it profiteth me nothing." I Corinthians 13:1-3

This scripture is talking about a circumstance wherein a believer can have faith and good works, but amount to nothing in God's sight.

What does it mean to be "nothing" in God's sight? Does that in any way suggest that one can be in right-standing with God?

No, nothing means *nothing*.

Why? Because love is the fulfillment of God's command to believers. Love is the fulfilling of the law. (Romans 13:8,10) No love, no obedience.

This is a strong statement, but the Word of God stands behind it: Without love there is no obedience to God's will.

With that said, let us take another look at the book of Matthew, where we see devastating glimpses of our Lord rejecting two groups of people who have not understood the true meaning of faith.

Witness again the horror of Matthew 7:21-23

"Not every one that saith unto me, Lord, Lord, shall enter into the kingdom of heaven; but he that doeth the will of my Father which is in heaven. Many will say to me in that day, Lord, Lord, have we not prophesied in thy name? and in thy name have cast out devils? and in thy name done many wonderful works? And then will I profess unto them, I never knew you: depart from me, ye that work iniquity."

Jesus is not singling out unbelievers here, people who during their lifetimes made no pretense of following Him. These people thought they were on the right path. Or if they did not think so, they at least thought being off the path would be excusable. Perhaps they thought that whatever they were doing in their lives had been acceptable to God, that their works would make them acceptable or that maybe grace would cover them.

The facts that (a.) they called Him Lord, and (b.) they performed scriptural works in His name, are two evidences that they were not just believers in Jesus, but that they also understood something about spiritual authority, and in fact, used that authority successfully. That authority is the name of Jesus, which He gave His followers to use. (Luke 10:19) By using the phrase, "in your name," the believers of Matthew 7 indicate they understood that Jesus gave His followers the authority to use His name, for in Mark 16:17, He said of believers, "*In My name they shall cast out devils.*" These people of Matthew 7 did not say they tried and failed to cast out devils, but actually did it.

On the other hand, we see unbelievers (in Acts 19:14-16) – Luke calls them "vagabond Jews, exorcists" – trying to cast out devils and failing miserably because they took it upon themselves *"to call over them which had evil spirits the name of the Lord Jesus, saying, We adjure you by Jesus whom Paul preacheth."*

These unbelievers recognized there was some sort of power and authority in the name of Jesus, but they had no true understanding of the authority Jesus gave His followers; they were trying to use the name of Jesus as though it were a spell to be cast. However, they had no *right* to use His name; He did not give it to them, but only to those who trust in Him. The words of the vagabond Jews proved their knowledge of Jesus was indirect – they knew *of* Him only through preaching or word of mouth, rather than in personal relationship.

Also note that the believers of Matthew 7 did what are considered, Biblically, to be good works. Jesus Himself cast out devils and His disciples cast them out, and because they did, unbelievers converted and became believers. Casting out devils is a good, scriptural thing to do. Yet, Jesus told these people of Matthew 7 to depart from Him because He had never known them. They thought they were in right relationship with Him. But neither the fact that they thought so, nor that they performed good works, could save them.

We can see that they believed in Jesus, they understood and accepted the authority He gave to His followers and they performed what appeared to be good works, but what we cannot see is their motivation for doing the works. Was their motive prestige, or money, to appear spiritual, to exalt themselves, to assuage and compensate for feelings of guilt, to draw great numbers of followers to themselves, to "earn" salvation or a position of righteousness with God? We are not told what their motivation was, but we can quickly determine what it was *not*.

Jesus said they worked iniquity. The Greek word for iniquity is *anomia* (an-om-ee'-ah), which means illegality, violation of law, wickedness or transgression of the law, and unrighteousness. Other translations say they practiced "lawlessness." So let's examine what lawlessness is.

Remember that the law according to Jesus is not a system of complicated rules and ordinances, but the kind of obedience from the heart that recognizes God's desires and wholeheartedly agrees with them.

"For this, Thou shalt not commit adultery, Thou shalt not kill, Thou shalt not steal, Thou shalt not bear false witness, Thou shalt not covet; and if there be any other commandment, it is briefly comprehended in this saying, namely, Thou shalt love thy neighbour as thyself. Love worketh no ill to his neighbour: therefore love is the fulfilling of the law." Romans 13:9-10

The law under the new covenant is fulfilled by love: loving God with our entire being, and loving our neighbors as ourselves. Obedience to this law produces the works God ordains and expects of us.

In other words, the intent of the law – i.e., living life without sin – was not obliterated by the coming of

Jesus. The fulfillment of the law was *made possible by Jesus*, and love is the fulfillment of that law.

Grace does not give anyone a license to break the "Old Testament" commandments, but provides the thankfulness of heart, and the love for God that motivates us to obey them from our hearts.

Without doing acts of obedience that are motivated by love for God and love for our neighbors, we cannot be said to be true followers of Christ, or true believers. *Love is the motivation that proves we are truly our Father's children.*

Thus, by viewing the failure of these Matthew 7 believers as a lack of obedience to God's law, we conclude that love was absent from their lives, since love is the fulfillment of the law. It appears that the people were doing works that, on the surface, seemed to be good works, but were not motivated by love for God and love for their neighbors.

Let me point out one last fact about the unsaved believers of Matthew 7. Note that Jesus said of them, *"I never knew you."*

Now, why did He say, *"I* never knew *you"* rather than, *"You* never knew *Me"*?

Most Christians who think these people were unbelievers would probably interpret Jesus's words to mean that they really did not know the Lord at all – in other words, that any commitment they might have made to Him was lip-service only. That's how we

Christians tend to define salvation: as *knowing the Lord.* Yet Jesus did not word it that way. He specifically said *He did not know them.*

Doesn't Jesus know all men? Doesn't He know the secrets of our hearts, and know our very thoughts? Of course! But He said He never knew the people in question because something was missing from the relationship. A key to understanding His use of that phrase is found in I Corinthians 8:3:

"But if any man love God, the same is known of him."

You see, you and I must love God before *we* can say we know Him in a meaningful, relational way. And what's more important, we must love Him before He can say *He knows us.* And again, this love with which we are to love Him is one that expresses itself in good works.

In his letter to the Galatians, Paul chastised those who were returning to the dead works of the law:

"But now, after that ye have known God, or rather are known of God, how turn ye again to the weak and beggarly elements, whereunto ye desire again to be in bondage?" Galatians 4:9 (Emphasis added)

There, he makes a distinction between our knowing God and God knowing us. His distinction seems to be that it is a rather higher privilege and state to be known by God than it is to know God. Many people might claim to know Him, but in truth, His knowledge of us, through our having given ourselves to Him, is of greater significance. In fact, our knowledge of Him will be shallow until we give ourselves over to His knowledge of our hearts.

If we do not love God, we are not known by Him. Since that is true, the inverse of the statement must also be true: that is, if we are not known by God, we do not love Him. Jesus said to the unsaved believers of Matthew 7, "I never knew you." According to I Corinthians 8:3, they could not have truly loved Jesus.

Paul made a similar distinction to Timothy:

"Nevertheless the foundation of God standeth sure, having this seal, The Lord knoweth them that are his. And, Let every one that nameth the name of Christ depart from iniquity." 2 Timothy 2:19

The foundation of God has a seal, Paul said. The Bible says that we are like a building, specifically, the temple of God. In fact it says our bodies are the temple of the Holy Spirit. The seal has been set in the most basic place, the foundation. In our day, many buildings are fixed with a seal, or plaque, upon its dedication, giving a specific time and reason for its dedication. Ephesians 2:20 says that, as the household of God, we are built on the foundation of the prophets and apostles, whose Chief Cornerstone is Jesus Christ. In fact, I Corinthians 3:11 shows us that the entire foundation is Jesus Christ, which includes the prophets and apostles because they themselves were founded upon Him. In Ephesians 1:13, we see that the Bible says we have been sealed with the Holy

Spirit. (See also Ephesians 4:30) The focal point of the seal is that the Lord knows those who belong to Him. If we claim to be His, the evidence that we have His seal (His knowing us) on our foundation is that we depart from sin.

The prophet Nahum is quoted as saying, "*The LORD is good, a strong hold in the day of trouble; and he knoweth them that trust in him.*" Nahum 1:7

The "day of trouble" turned out to be the Day of Judgment for the people of Matthew 7. They could not fool God. They fooled only themselves. God knew those who were His. How crucial it is for us to know we are His rather than to trust a superficial understanding of God's will! And how better to know than to make sure He knows us – every hidden sin, every secret, every carnal part of our hearts!

We have heard people boast of knowing a celebrity, but have seen that such knowledge was shallow unless the celebrity also knew them.

How can you know someone who doesn't know you? And how can you have faith in One you really don't know? Being known by Him, then, is of utmost importance.

Let the Holy Spirit bring light into all areas of your being. I John 1:7 says, "*if we walk in the light, as he is in the light, we have fellowship one with another, and the blood of Jesus Christ his Son cleanseth us from all sin.*"

He is able to keep that which we commit to Him. (See 2 Timothy 1:12) Therefore, we must commit ourselves to Him entirely, not in part. He cannot keep what we do not commit to Him. Paul said, "*I pray God your whole spirit and soul and body be preserved blameless unto the coming of our Lord Jesus Christ.*" (I Thessalonians 5:23)

This truth is one that we do not ordinarily express in our Christian vernacular; namely that it is just as vital in our relationship with Jesus Christ that He know us as it is that we know Him. Our vernacular tends to focus only on whether one knows Jesus Christ, to the exclusion of the obverse.

Yes, we must know Him through His Word and through fellowship with Him. No question that we must know Him! But we can be very wrong in our thinking if our efforts at following Christ are directed only toward knowing Him and we fail to reveal our hearts to Him. I have met people who base their entire knowledge of Christ on one-time acts of partial commitment:

They "joined the church" once, or have always attended faithfully.

They raised their hand in church in response to a pastor's appeal

They read the Bible from cover to cover once.

They were baptized as a child.

They "belong" to a particular sect or denomination.

Any relationship must be based on meaningful two-way communication. Those who look to fulfill only the superficial requirements of "being a Christian," with the possible motive of escaping hellfire while still living a life focused on pleasing themselves, might easily convince themselves that they know Him and/or that He knows them. Neither reading the Bible, going to church, raising a hand during an altar call, giving money, or "joining" the church means we have a love relationship with God through Christ. (More about this in Chapter Nine) In basing our salvation on a one-time act or partial commitment, we would miss the fact that God's commandments to us are summed up in all-out love for Him, accompanied by love for our neighbors that equals the love we have for ourselves.

The apostle John said, *"He that saith, I know him, and keepeth not his commandments, is a liar, and the truth is not in him."* (I John 2:4)

However, if we direct our efforts at having Him know us *as well as* at knowing Him, then we will place equal focus on accessing His heart and giving Him full access to our hearts, our inner lives, to correct us and change us into people who will glorify Him in all that we do, thus, loving Him and obeying Him fully. We will make it our goal to have Him be pleased with us and our lives. Giving God full access to the secret places of your heart is what is known as living a life of repentance. It acknowledges that we are flawed and that in our flesh dwells no good thing, yet it also acknowledges that He will purify our hearts as we submit ourselves fully to His correction and instruction.

In other words, our aim at being in right relationship with God should be directed beyond our own interests and fully to His. If we do not extend our hope and vision for faith's purposes beyond ourselves – i.e., if we only focus on what we *should* be doing instead of what He *wants* us to be doing – we can fail to bring all our focus on pleasing Him. Remember, it is not the doing of the works that pleases God, but the doing of them through the motive of a deep abiding love for Him and our neighbors.

Now let's take another look at a second example of people who thought they were saved but, unfortunately, found out otherwise:

"Then shall he say also unto them on the left hand, Depart from me, ye cursed, into everlasting fire, prepared for the devil and his angels: For I was an hungred, and ye gave me no meat: I was thirsty, and ye gave me no drink: I was a stranger, and ye took me not in: naked, and ye clothed me not: sick, and in prison, and ye visited me not. Then shall they also answer him, saying, Lord, when saw we thee an hungred, or athirst, or a stranger, or naked, or sick, or in prison, and did not minister unto thee? Then shall he answer them, saying, Verily I say unto you, Inasmuch as ye did it not to one of the least of these, ye did it not to me. And these shall go away into

everlasting punishment: but the righteous into life eternal." Matthew 25:41-46

These disobedient people – "goats" according to verse 33 – like the people of Matthew 7, called Jesus Lord. They had that much faith, but they had no ordinary works of love and compassion to show for their lives on earth. They did not recognize Jesus in common, needy people, nor did they respond with the love of God. With whatever things they busied themselves during their lives, they failed miserably because of the omission of an absolutely essential ingredient: love, as expressed through good works.

Eighteenth century evangelist George Whitefield said of the obedient ones, the "sheep" of Matthew 25, on the other hand, "It is evident that the people did not depend upon these good actions for their justification in the sight of God. 'When saw we thee an hungered,' they say, 'and fed thee or thirsty, and gave thee drink?...' The language they used and the questions they asked are quite improper for persons who are relying on their own righteousness for acceptance and innocence in the sight of God."

In other words, the "sheep" of Matthew 25 seemed to have a right relationship with God, in that their works were an outgrowth of their love for God and love for their neighbors rather than as an attempt at justifying themselves before God and men.

Whitefield concludes, "they were so far from depending on their works for justification in the sight of God that they were filled, as it were, with a holy blushing to think our Lord would condescend to mention, much more to reward them for, their poor works of faith and labors of love."

Their works were simply an evidence of the love of God in their hearts, while the lack of works demonstrated by the "goats" was a lack of that same evidence.

Likewise, in the parable of Lazarus and the rich man, why was the rich man rejected? He was a Jew, we know because he refers to Abraham as "Father Abraham," and Abraham calls him "son." Apparently, he was rejected because he did not share his abundance with Lazarus. That is, he did not let the love of God move him to reach out to others. (See Luke 16:20-25)

In neither case did Jesus say He rejected these people because they did not "BELIEVE" in Him.

We could say that these examples demonstrate the inability of works alone or faith alone to save us. But because both groups (Matthew 7 and 25) had at least a lip-service relationship with the Lord, we must ask the question, Are faith and works *together* adequate?

And again, we must conclude they are not. Obedience to God's command to love must be the motive that keeps faith and works of obedience scriptural.

Consider these words of John:

"But whoso hath this world's good, and seeth his brother have need, and shutteth up his bowels of compassion from him, how dwelleth the love of God in him?" I John 3:17

In the 13th chapter of I Corinthians, we find a list of things – including faith and various works – that would tend to make many people feel very spiritual and acceptable to God, yet which are absolutely meaningless without love at their core. Take a close look at the list below. Ask yourself if doing or possessing one or more of these might give you a good feeling about having served God well, about knowing Him or having Him know you:

Speaking in tongues (of men and of angels)

Having the gift of prophecy

Understanding all mysteries and all knowledge

Having faith strong enough to move mountains

Bestowing all your goods to feed the poor

Giving your body to be burned

Don't kid yourself. If you understood all mysteries, you might think you were one of God's highly favored people. Likewise, if you spoke to a mountain and commanded it to move – *and it DID!* – you would be just like any other human. You would be tempted to think you were in very close relationship with God.

Nevertheless, even though you could claim all of these as your gifts or acts, if you did not have the love of God, and love *for* God, motivating your actions, you would be ZERO to God.

If you read the remainder of I Corinthians 13 along with Luke 6, you find out just what kind of love by which we are to be motivated.

It is the kind of love that motivates believers to show love to our enemies and to do good to those who hate us, to endure all things, never behave rudely or seek our own way, to do good and lend, hoping for nothing in return, to forgive, to be merciful, to refrain from condemning others and to give liberally. (See Luke 6:27-38)

Paul and John agree, then, that love is essential to works and faith. Like the beautiful car mentioned in Chapter Three, faith and works alone are missing the essential element that make them useful, in this case, to God.

In point of fact, the three are absolutely essential to each other.

CHAPTER SEVEN

The Inseparable Marriage

So, what is the inescapable conclusion of the ground we have covered?

Faith needs works. And both faith and works need love.

Faith, works and love are bonded together as though by molecular structure, just like the water molecule we discussed in Chapter Three. They exist in "irreducible complexity," to borrow biochemist Michael Behe's term. Each is what I call a *sine qua non* for the others.

In the diagram above, I use the word "WORKS." Because it is linked with love and faith, you may assume the works are good works, and that "works" is interchangeable with obedience to God, or acts of obedience.

"Put on therefore, as God's elect, holy and beloved, a heart of compassion, kindness, lowliness, meekness,

longsuffering; forbearing one another, and forgiving each other, if any man have a complaint against any; even as the Lord forgave you, so also do ye: and above all these things put on love, which is the bond of perfectness." Colossians 3:12-14

Scriptural faith can only be achieved in a composite form, as depicted in the drawing. Believing, without corroborating works, is dead faith. Works alone are an attempt to circumvent grace. And even faith that produces works is insufficient unless the works have the proper motivation within them.

Accepting and understanding this interrelationship will be difficult for some because they have been suckled on the idea that faith is simplistic.

The simple truth of faith is that when you truly love God, you will believe in and trust Him, and you will want to obey Him by doing the works that please Him. That is simple. However, faith is not *simplistic*. To say something is simplistic is to say it is characterized by a false simplicity that ignores complicating factors. Simplistic belief amounts to nothing more than intellectually accepting the fact that God raised Jesus from the dead. Truly believing "on the Lord Jesus Christ," according to Acts 16:31, involves the scriptural kind of belief that is rooted and grounded in love, producing obedience to the scriptural injunction to do good works. If you believe in that manner, *"thou shalt be saved, and thy house."*

Love is so integral to faith that it cannot be removed without destroying the concept. Love was God's motive for saving us. He loved us so much that He gave His only begotten Son that we might be saved.

If you sense in yourself a resistance to this knowledge, perhaps because of traditional thinking about faith, take this to God in prayer. Ask Him to show you truth. If you don't presently have a love for truth, ask Him to give you a sincere love for His truth. Never hold on to notions that are not grounded in God's Word, but seek truth with a solid scriptural foundation, as confirmed by the teaching of the Holy Spirit.

Your zealous love for truth is critical. No matter who brings information to you about scripture – be it a parent, a respected teacher, a pastor, or the author of this book – you have a scriptural injunction to bring it before the Holy Spirit in personal study of the scriptures involved. In something as important as faith, it is essential that your and my understanding be entirely founded upon the Word of God as taught by the Holy Spirit. *(Author's note: Please forgive the repetition. Being repetitive is worth the risk of annoying some when souls are in the balance.)*

We know that without faith it is impossible to please God (Hebrews 11:6). And the Bible makes it clear that if we do believe on the Lord Jesus Christ, we will be saved (Acts 16:31) But we have also seen that faith goes beyond mere intellectual assent.

"If anyone is in Christ, he is a new creature; old things are passed away and behold, all things have become new." 2 Corinthians 5:17

This scripture tells us a change will take place in us if we are truly in Christ. Old things will pass away: that is, the old sinful lifestyle will not remain.

Let's examine faith, works and love as three points of a triangle and review each interrelationship in light of scripture to see if they are indeed inseparable.

The Faith-Works Link

When Jesus told Nicodemus, *"You must be born again,"* (John 3:7) He was referring not to a symbolic act, but to a total spiritual transformation brought about by the indwelling of the Holy Spirit. Belief in Christ leads us to be born again, and that transformation leads us into a radical change of lifestyle.

Yes, being born again does "reposition" us in Christ in a way that we cannot necessarily see, because He has made us to *"sit together in heavenly places in Christ."* (Ephesians 2:6) So there is an element of transformation that is invisible to us. But there is also the real and practical transformation of indwelling by the Holy Spirit, Who radically changes the life and lifestyle of the one being indwelt.

That change in lifestyle is part of what James referred to when he said, *"faith without works is dead."* James makes it clear that if we do not follow up our hearing of the Word of God with obedience to it, we enter into deceit (see 1:22 below). Self-deceit. We fool ourselves into thinking that, having heard the truth and believed it, we have done all that God wants us to do. James makes the bold statement that even the devils believe (2:19), so that belief alone is not what makes up genuine faith.

"But be ye doers of the word, and not hearers only, deceiving your own selves." James 1:22

"But wilt thou know, O vain man, that faith without works is dead?" James 2:20

"For as the body without the spirit is dead, so faith without works is dead also." James 2:26

"For we are his workmanship, created in Christ Jesus unto good works, which God hath before ordained that we should walk in them." Ephesians 2:10

Works validate faith, they perfect it (James 2:22) and help prevent self-deception. Now, immediately, you might say, "Works did not prevent the people of Matthew 7 from being deceived into thinking they were saved!" And you would be right. Not only does faith require works in order to be genuine, but works need love to make them *good* works, as we have already seen.

What are works, then?

Genuine good works and obedience are virtually synonymous in the context of Scripture. They are acts of obedience to God. They glorify God. Works that do not glorify God are "wood, hay and stubble." (I Corinthians 3:12) And just as faith without works is dead, so works without the love of God are dead. Dead works. According to Hebrews 6:1, repentance from dead works is foundational to our walk with Christ. The only works we as sinners were capable of in our unregenerated lives were dead works, because we did not have the love of God in us.

As sinners, we might have called our works good, and to the outward appearance, they might have seemed to many non-believers and believers alike to be good. But the defining criterion for genuine good works is whether they are pleasing to God, being a loving response to the urging of His will.

Paul told the Galatians to "*walk in the Spirit, and ye shall not fulfill the lust of the flesh.*" Our works of obedience to God's Word and His Holy Spirit are the starting point in our walk of faith.

Good works include the kinds of works Jesus Himself performed: laying hands on the sick, casting out devils and preaching the good news (the gospel) to those around us. Don't be surprised that God wants you to do these kinds of things. Jesus said as much in the last verses of Mark chapter 16, and concluded that they were among the signs that would "*follow them that believe*" – another confirmation that works "follow" faith. It is instructive that He did not say that only the apostles, elders or full-time ministers would do these works, but that "*those who believe*" would do them.

In another place, Jesus said, "*He that believeth on Me, the works that I do shall he do also; and greater works than these shall he do; because I go unto My Father.*" (John 14:12)

Good works also include "alms deeds," which are acts of kindness to the poor. Luke tells of a disciple named Tabitha who "*was full of good works and almsdeeds,*" (Acts 9:36) including making coats for widows (v. 39). Widows "*of good works*" are described in Titus 5:10 as those women who have reared children, lodged strangers, washed the feet of the saints and relieved the afflicted.

Jesus commended the "sheep" of Matthew 25 for feeding the hungry, giving drink to the thirsty, clothing the naked, visiting the sick and imprisoned, and taking in strangers.

The truth is, if you really want to do the good works of God, it is not difficult to discern from the scriptures what kind of works those are or to find opportunities to do them.

So, by the scriptures above, you see that faith and works are inseparable. The point that needs to be made here is that works are not optional. They are essential. No works, no obedience. No obedience, no faith.

Now let's take a look at works and love.

The Works-Love Link

One caution about doing works is this: Do not do them to be seen and praised by others or to gain righteousness. (Matthew 6:1-7) Such selfish motives pretending to be obedience are an affront to God. We are to do our works (acts of obedience) in secret as much as possible, to ensure we will not be glorified by men. If we honor God with that kind of selflessness, He will reward us openly. Love is the critical ingredient of works, and God's kind of love is directed toward others and their welfare. If we are motivated by a desire to "earn points" with God, meaning to garner for ourselves a degree of righteousness and acceptability in His sight, then our works are nothing more than the stench of filthy rags to Him. (Isaiah 64:6) Why? Because Jesus paid the price for us to be acceptable in God's presence. That was God's sacrificial gift to us. We cannot and must not try to subvert that sacrifice with a dependence upon works of our own. The works that we do are expected to be an outgrowth of love and thankfulness for what God *has done* for us through Jesus. If our purpose in doing works is to give the appearance to people that we are righteous, then we know from the scriptures that their praise or recognition is all the reward we will receive.

Jesus told His disciples, *"If you love Me, keep My commandments."* (John 14:15) All good works – that is, acts of love toward our neighbors and love toward God – are acts of obedience, because His commandments are to love. By this scripture, Jesus indicated that works of obedience are a response to our love for Him. Works spring from that kind of love. Just as we can say, "No obedience, no faith," we can also say, "No obedience, no love," and vice versa.

He also said, *"If you keep My commandments, you will abide in My love."* That focuses on the effect that our obedience produces – that of keeping us in His love. To abide means to make one's habitation, or dwelling place. And the apostle John went a step further saying, if one will obey the scriptures, *"the love of God is perfected in Him."* (I John 2:5)

Conversely, if we do not obey God's Word, we do not love Him. And as obedience breeds greater love, and perfects love in us, disobedience breeds nothing but self-deception and disrespect for the Lord.

"He that hath my commandments, and keepeth them, he it is that loveth me: and he that loveth me shall be loved of my Father, and I will love him, and will manifest myself to him." John 14:21

"If ye keep my commandments, ye shall abide in my love; even as I have kept my Father's commandments, and abide in his love." John 15:10

"But whoso keepeth his word, in him verily is the love of God perfected: hereby know we that we are in him." I John 2:5

"For this is the love of God, that we keep his commandments: and his commandments are not grievous." I John 5:3

"And this is love, that we walk after his commandments. This is the commandment, That, as ye have heard from the beginning, ye should walk in it." II John 1:6

"He that saith, I know him, and keepeth not his commandments, is a liar, and the truth is not in him." I John 2:4

In the book of Revelation, Jesus commanded that the church of Ephesus be warned:

"I know thy works, and thy labour, and thy patience, and how thou canst not bear them which are evil: and thou hast tried them which say they are apostles, and are not, and hast found them liars: And hast borne, and hast patience, and for my name's sake

hast labored, and hast not fainted. Nevertheless I have somewhat against thee, because thou hast left thy first love. Remember therefore from whence thou art fallen, and repent, and do the first works; or else I will come unto thee quickly, and will remove thy candlestick out of his place, except thou repent."
Revelation 2:1-5

He was telling the Church at Ephesus that, yes, they still had works, but that something had happened to their works. Their first works were fired by love, and though they continued to do works, their latter works missed the mark because they were not motivated by love. He told them to repent of doing works that did not have love as their motive.

Works can become rote, routine, even drudgery when we shift into a mode of doing them out of obligation, a sense of duty, as "part of my job" or to assuage guilt feelings. Or worse, they can be self-righteous acts that seek to supplant the righteousness of Jesus as our only entrance into God's presence.

I should not fail to point out the obvious here. That is, Jesus gave us two simple commandments: Love the Lord your God with all your heart, and with all your soul, and with all your mind, and with all your strength...and love your neighbor as yourself. *"On these two commandments,"* He said, *"hang all the law and prophets."* (Matthew 22:40)

Therefore, it is impossible to keep His commandments if we do not love.

The Love-Faith Link

By now it should be clear that faith must produce works of obedience or die, and that works must be motivated by love or be dead works. Now you need to know that the only thing that makes faith work is love. In other words, faith needs the love of God in order to work. That is what Paul told the Galatians (5:6)

"For in Jesus Christ neither circumcision availeth any thing, nor uncircumcision; but faith which worketh by love."

That statement by Paul reveals that through Jesus, circumcision of the flesh – which is a work of the law – was rendered meaningless, and in effect, was replaced by faith that works by love. Another way to paraphrase that without harming the meaning is: Prior to Jesus, circumcision of the flesh was the act of obedience to the law that once signified trust in God; it no longer is meaningful. Now your faith in Jesus Christ is what is meaningful to God. That faith becomes genuine as your love for Him produces works of obedience to Him.

The love of God in us produces workable faith, genuine faith. And because it is faith that is born out of love, works produced by that faith are works of love.

The sacrifice Jesus made for us ought to cause such a profound gratefulness in each of us that we are moved to love Him and believe in Him enough to follow Him in the new life He provided for us.

Again, faith that is not founded in love is empty and meaningless:

"...if I have the gift of prophecy, and know all mysteries and all knowledge, and if I have all faith, so as to remove mountains, but have not love, I am nothing." I Corinthians 13:2

Just as belief has its simplistic meaning, which is a counterfeit of the genuine, and just as counterfeit (dead) works exist, not fitting the scriptural definition of good works, so does love have its counterfeit that bears no resemblance to the kind of love (Greek: *agape*) prescribed by God's Word.

For example, many use the word *love* to mean enjoy – e.g., "I love hiking. I love chocolate ice cream." That word is akin to the Greek word *thelo* (thel'-o) that Jesus used in Mark 12:38 to say, *"Beware of the scribes, which love to go in long clothing, and love salutations in the marketplaces."* Even though people love (*thelo*) to say they love things, actions and conditions, such use of that "*love*" falls far short of the kind of love we are focusing on in this chapter, and only tends toward confusion in some circles.

Just as cults have devised "another Jesus" to be the centerpiece for their services, there are groups who call on the name of Jesus, but who operate by a sticky, self-indulgent and even new-age kind of counterfeit "love," rather than the kind of love described in I Corinthians 13 and Luke 6.

I once visited a church that touted love as its focal point. I recall that the congregation was given to much hugging between members, and polite, smiling greetings toward visitors. The service had a sweet and peaceful nature about it that seemed to me to be skin deep. I don't recall hearing much about Jesus Christ during the service. When a baby was "baptized" in rose petals, I began to suspect the love angle was a performance based on a kind of love that simulates the scriptural kind of love.

At best, the kind of love being expressed in such a circumstance is *Philadelphos* or *phileo* (Greek for brotherly love) and used to describe fondness or affection between friends. Of course, brotherly love is a good and very natural thing. It may be the highest form of natural love. But it is not an absolute love. *Phileo* can have qualifications to it. Judas expressed a form of *phileo* love when he kissed Jesus in betrayal. The word "kiss" in Luke 22:47 is the same Greek word, *phileo*, used to describe brotherly love.

In recent decades, so-called churches have surfaced in America that openly violate the edicts of scripture and the clear injunctions of Jesus Christ, rationalizing that God does not judge acts such as homosexuality or fornication if they are performed in a "love" relationship. People in congregations devoted to their own carnal version of love deceive themselves. Their misuse of the word *love* is in reality a substitute or euphemism for *lust*, and amounts to dishonesty and mockery of God. They do not fear God, and perhaps justify the absence of fear with the scripture, "*Perfect love casts out all fear.*" (I John 4:18) However, perfect love reverences and honors God and His Word, and fears purposely disobeying Him.

The fear of which the apostle John spoke is a fear of being judged. In context, he said, "*Herein is our love made perfect, that we may have boldness in the day of judgment: because as he is, so are we in this world. There is no fear in love; but perfect love casteth out fear: because fear hath torment. He that feareth is not made perfect in love.*"

In other words, because we walk in love as Jesus did, we will have no fear of judgment on Judgment Day. However, that does not mean we've lost reverential fear of and respect for Him. We must reverence Him and fear His chastisement if we are to remain obedient. Being chastised by God is not something we delight in.

Indeed, even evangelical ministers may think that loving God dispenses with the need for fearing Him.

The love that is being discussed in this book – love that results in obedience to the will of God – does not negate a realistic fear of being disobedient to Him, a holiness-producing fear.

Paul wrote to Timothy, "*Them that sin rebuke before all, that others also may fear.*" (1Timothy 5:20) And Psalms 103:13 says, "*Just as a father has compassion on his children, so the Lord has compassion on those who fear Him.*"

I recall a great book entitled *The Fear of the Lord*, by a minister named John Bevere. In it he said, "We will soon learn that we cannot truly love God until we fear Him; nor can we truly fear Him until we love Him."

Some things have an appearance of godly love, but, without a desire to glorify Jesus Christ at their center and without a supporting basis in His Word, as well as a holy, reverential fear for Him, they are no more than misunderstandings about God's love at best, and perversions of it, at worst.

Of the various kinds of love expressible in the Greek language of the New Testament, the highest one to which we are called is *agape* (ah-gah'-pay). Some translations of the Bible render that word as "charity," while others call it "love." In addition to love and charity, meanings given by Strong's Concordance for *agape* include "affection or benevolence." Using the word, "charity," could present problems because, as we use the word "believe" with many meanings, we in America sometimes filter the word *charity* through a limited understanding as a type of altruistic work or giving that is common in secular vernacular. It would be easy for someone to mistakenly believe that giving "to charity" out of some motivation other than love – say, for the purpose of a tax deduction – would satisfy God's call for His people to express *agape* to their neighbors.

What would motivate a believer to bypass love and still try to "fit into the mold" of being a Christian?

I don't believe anyone who is fully aware of the consequences would purposely avoid love as a motivation in serving God. Most in that situation, I believe, would be there due to a lack of understanding. Failing to love God and love one's neighbors as oneself while going through the motions of Christian life is essentially giving lip-service to God.

I believe it begins with an unwillingness to die to Self, which is the original god of each person's universe. If that condition persists and the Holy Spirit is unable to break through to the inner person to communicate the basic understanding of being crucified with Christ, the individual will in all likelihood consider himself a completed work that needs no transformation. He will be okay in his own eyes, seeing no need to deny himself a lifestyle that goes against the dictates of scripture. That person will not be likely to consider the Bible as God's personal word of instruction to him.

Seeing no need to be transformed, as Romans 12 instructs us, such a self-willed and self-directed person will tend to allow himself whatever indulgences of the flesh he considers acceptable for a social Christian, without submitting to the Holy Spirit for guidance or correction. That person will probably either take lightly the injunction to study to show oneself approved unto God, and will probably find sanctuary in a group of believers who are cool to lukewarm in their approach to the gospel.

In such a group you might find people who see the church primarily as a place to network, a place for making beneficial contacts and finding social interaction. Here you might find politically minded folk who see Christians as voters, necessary for their personal support, and the Word of God as a decent set of homilies or a source for a good quote.

Many people whom society exalts as philanthropists may fool themselves into thinking that, when they give, they are winning the approval of God and gaining some supposed goodness of soul. They are greatly deceived if their motivation is primarily personal PR, tax deductibility or to gain political influence. The sober truth is, again, that works do not buy us right-standing with God. Only a personal commitment to following Jesus Christ can put us in right relationship with God. Even Cornelius, the soldier introduced in Acts 10, whose prayers and charitable deeds had "*come up for a memorial before God*" and who "feared God," still had to be converted as a follower of Christ in order to be accepted by God, as was evidenced once Peter preached the gospel to him. His love and fear for God did not "buy" him salvation; it perhaps conditioned him for salvation by Jesus Christ.

The original Greek words used to express *love* in the New Testament were actually insufficient to describe the kind of love our God has for us. And of course, that is an understatement. No language can adequately encapsulate the attributes of God. Therefore, Paul expanded on the meaning of God's variety of love through I Corinthians 13, to make it more nearly accurate.

Using the word, *agape*, Paul describes it as the kind of love:

- that suffers (endures) long and is kind

- that does not envy

- that does not vaunt itself (boast)

- that is not puffed up

- does not behave itself unseemly

- does not seek its own well-being to the exclusion of others'

- is not easily provoked

- does not think evil

- does not rejoice in iniquity, but rejoices in the truth

- bears all things, hopes all things, and endures all things

I am sure you know that, just because you are inhabited by the Holy Spirit, acting in *agape* love toward God and others does not come automatically. You must actively allow the Holy Spirit to change you and lead you into reproducing God's love. Paul wrote, *"As many as are led by the Spirit of God, these are the sons of God."*

No matter how hard one may try to force some other kind of love into the mold of scriptural love – *agape* – it will not fit.

All that is to say, there are counterfeits in secular life for every essential element of God's salvation.

There is a faith that exists without good works or scriptural love, but that is not genuine faith

There is a kind of works that exists without faith in God's Word, and that stands apart from the love of God, but this kind of works cannot be classified as good works or obedience to God's will.

And there is a kind of love that exists apart from God's kind, a love that is not born of faith in God's Word and does not produce obedience to His will. Such love is not the kind of love to which God has called us.

What people often miss is the fact that it is *agape* love that makes our faith work and our obedience genuine.

Do not lean to your own understanding when it comes to the characteristics of God that are meant to be in your life. You must apply your heart to understanding them by the Spirit of God as intended in the Word of God.

To miss them in meaning is to miss them entirely.

And now it is time to learn that we can enter into the fullness of what God expects of you and me, even though it seems to be an impossible assignment.

CHAPTER EIGHT

The Impossible Call

Don't be discouraged by the description of faith you have just read.

The ordinary person who sincerely examines himself will come to the conclusion that to live and walk in the kind of faith, love and works that have been described in these few chapters is an impossible dream.

Granted, that is a valid conclusion. *For man*, it is impossible.

But take note that it is not unlike God to require and expect the impossible of His sons and daughters, for only then can His power and glory be made known. God has called us to do the impossible through Him.

"And he said, The things which are impossible with men are possible with God." Luke 18:27

All things are possible with God.

Watchman Nee addressed the issue when he evaluated the reaction of the rich young ruler mentioned in Luke chapter 18. The words of Jesus quoted above were spoken immediately after He saw that the rich ruler became sorrowful at Jesus's injunction to him. He was sorrowful because, when he asked Jesus what he should do to inherit eternal life,

Jesus responded that he should sell all he owned, give it to the poor and "come, follow Me." Read an excerpt from that account:

"And when he heard this, he was very sorrowful: for he was very rich. And when Jesus saw that he was very sorrowful, he said, How hardly shall they that have riches enter into the kingdom of God! For it is easier for a camel to go through a needle's eye, than for a rich man to enter into the kingdom of God. And they that heard it said, Who then can be saved? And he said, The things which are impossible with men are possible with God." Luke 18: 23-27

In his book, *A Living Sacrifice*, Watchman Nee said of the young man, "He ought not to have sorrowfully departed. Man's failure is not due to his weakness, but to his not accepting God's strength. ...Our Lord wanted to prove to the young ruler what God can do, but he, instead, went away with the conclusion that the thing was impossible to him."

The truth is, there is much we cannot do when we focus on our human abilities and weaknesses. But just as the young ruler could have humbled himself and asked Jesus to give him the power and will to obey in selling all he owned and to give it to the poor, we, too, can do the impossible. Only, we must not walk away discouraged when we face seemingly impossible urgings from the Holy Spirit. We must humble ourselves to God, admit we cannot in our human-ness walk in faith, love and works, as He has prescribed, and ask Him to enable us to do so by His power and ability.

You might be stymied by the idea that God is requiring you to be perfect. If so, that could cause you to walk away from God, sorrowful that you cannot live up to what He expects. I have met a few people who did just that, rejecting the exhortation that God can and will enable them to be and do all that He asks of them.

A number of people I have shared the good news of Jesus Christ with sounded truly sad that they could not live up to God's expectations of them. We can tell them clearly and with compassion that God will accept them as they are and will enable them to change into the image He prescribes for them, but it's often difficult for them to squelch the old script running through their heads that, in the end, they are incapable.

Despite the miraculous change wrought by the indwelling presence of the Holy Spirit in the life of a born-again follower of Christ, the kind of love meant here does not come naturally. On the contrary, it comes supernaturally. The degree to which you give the Holy Spirit control in your life, the more "natural" the submission to love and obedience seems to be. Likewise, the less control you allow the Holy Spirit in your life, the more impossible the task will seem to love the way God desires. Regardless of how natural it might seem, the change comes only supernaturally.

Change is the basis of life in Christ, of course, meaning the complete change of a born-again spirit. Without that re-birth or regeneration in Jesus Christ, you will never be able to live up to the Christian life. People may acknowledge Jesus Christ as the Son of God and Savior of the world, even call Him Lord and attend church services religiously, but through it all, fail or refuse to give their entire lives over to Him in commitment. If you are among these, you will find it impossible to love God with all your heart, mind, soul and strength and to love your neighbor as yourself until you throw yourself upon His mercy, His grace and His ability and believe He can enable you to give up all for Him.

Once again, please understand that it is God's strength, ability and power He makes available to us. It is our own strength, ability and power from which He has saved us.

Jesus said, *"Be ye therefore perfect, even as your Father which is in heaven is perfect."* Matthew 5:48

Perfect, here, means to be mature in Christ, to be complete and grown up into His likeness.

Realize that He does not expect you to conjure up perfection from within yourself; He expects you to display His perfection, His perfect love. As you call on Him to supply you with impossible love, you are actually saying to Him that you want to die to yourself – your own insufficient abilities – and to take on His power and character.

Do that regularly and you will begin to see that the impossible is truly possible with Him.

I understand that some reading this book may be new believers in Christ, and could feel stronger than most the inability of their flesh to live up to the love of God. Just do not fear; God is faithful. He doesn't expect you to grow immediately to maturity, but do remain faithful in your trust of His Word and His Holy Spirit. As He shows you what He wants to change in you, submit to His instruction. Confess to Him anything in your heart that you may have hidden from others, that may cause you shame. Give Him access to your inner feelings, and let Him be the Teacher, Counselor, Guide and Healer. If you fail in your attempts to obey Him, run to Him instead of away from Him.

1 John 1:9 says, *"If we confess our sins, he is faithful and just to forgive us our sins, and to cleanse us from all unrighteousness."* He is gracious to forgive and cleanse us, and to carry us through temptations and trials.

No human asserting his own abilities to the uttermost limits can live up to the call to love God and others the way He defines love in I Corinthians 13 and in Luke 6. Yet that does not release us from the call to do it. It is such an impossibility that we must die to ourselves in order to obey the command. We must become as little children, without agendas, without guile, with only the will and ability to trust in God's higher power.

Perhaps the strongest enemy opposing your love of God and your love of your neighbors is inordinate love you have for yourself. Self-love will often manifest itself in an abiding sense that others are wrong and you are right, that they are faulty and you are endowed with extraordinary ability to correct their faulty thinking or actions. That turns out to be a fair definition of self-righteousness, as well. And interestingly, if you look deeper at self-love and self-righteousness, you see that the one whose will is exalted above all others in them is Self – which is an acceptable description of idolatry.

Self-love must be put in the proper perspective, which is that our wills must bow to the will of God. Our love for ourselves must never rival our love for God, and in fact must be far lower than our love for God, and no higher than our love for our neighbors. Self-righteousness must be abandoned for the righteousness that can only be gained through submission to Jesus Christ. And idolatry of Self must be vanquished completely.

We must choose daily to crucify the Self, the flesh, for which love (*agape*) is an impossible task, and commit to doing the impossible. Hear what Jesus said to his disciples:

"If any man will come after me, let him deny himself, and take up his cross, and follow me. For whosoever will save his life shall lose it: and whosoever will lose his life for my sake shall find it. For what is a man profited, if he shall gain the whole world, and lose his

own soul? or what shall a man give in exchange for his soul?" Matthew 16:24-26

The rich young ruler may not have been as bound by his riches as he was by the "impossible." He had only to ask for God's ability where his own was insufficient.

Let us not any longer be bound by those things that are impossible for us.

Our own righteousness (ability to act in rightness or in morally virtuous ways) is "as filthy rags." (Isaiah 64:6)

Whether the impossibility is in believing, loving or obeying, be assured that God will supply what we lack if we will only ask in faith, believing.

So what must you do if you realize you are not able to follow Jesus in the way He expects?

Do what your human nature wants *not* to do. Confess your sins and sinful nature to God (Who knows all anyway), and ask Jesus to forgive you. Give Him your life entirely, considering your life, as you have known it, to be over – as though at that moment you had suddenly died. Commit to living the balance of your life through Jesus alone; that is, live as though you are being kept on life support by the indwelling presence of God, through His grace, and that your daily sustenance and energy source is His Word, His life-giving breath and His voice.

If you do, you will experience what Jesus said He came to give – that is, life "more abundantly." John 10:10

CHAPTER NINE

The Importance of Motivation

So, what does all this mean in practical terms?

As Jesus demonstrated in Matthew 7, many who presume they are saved are not!

Probably, that basic fact does not come as a great surprise, but the difficulty is, we each think it means that someone else is fooled into thinking he is saved. It could not be you or me.

Yet, once again, we must examine our faith.

"Examine yourselves, whether ye be in the faith; prove your own selves. Know ye not your own selves, how that Jesus Christ is in you, except ye be reprobates?" 2 Corinthians 13:5

Many are hearers of the Word, but not doers, deceiving themselves. They may even have a lip-service love for God. But the absence of true love and good works negates their faith.

Others truly love God, but, without knowledge of His Word or His will they cannot have genuine faith. God went to great lengths to get the gospel to the centurion, Cornelius. That man's love for God motivated him to pray earnestly and give alms. Yet, had he never heard the gospel, faith could not have come to him. He – even with all his love for God – would have been incomplete.

Still others may do works expressly prescribed by Jesus (e.g., Matthew 7), but with the motivation of earning righteousness or of wanting the praise of men for themselves. They might have mountain-moving faith, but lack heart-moving faith. The absence of *agape* love as motivation will cause works that appear to be good works on the surface to become as a sounding brass or a tinkling cymbal.

As David told his son Solomon, *"The Lord searches all hearts and understands all the intent of the thoughts."* I Chronicles 28.9

The implications of all you've read here about the true definition of faith are dramatic. If you have never heard your pastor or anyone else define faith in terms of obedience and *agape* love, ask yourself why.

Have they preached it, though you missed it through dullness of hearing? With all due respect to pastors and other ministers, they are not infallible.

Have you never heard it because you've been attending the wrong congregation(s)?

Or have you simply stayed away from other believers altogether, opting for the convenience of television or recordings as your means of discipleship?

Have you been acting out a relationship with God that treats Him like a dead relative? Or perhaps, acting out a relationship that ignores His Word in favor of beliefs you *hope* are true?

Have you spent more time in the world and worldliness than with God and godliness?

Or maybe you have worshiped tradition.

The disciples of Jesus asked Him to tell about the end of the world. One of the signs He gave that indicated the end of the world was near was, *"Because lawlessness is increased, the love of many will grow cold."* (Matthew 24:12) Again, I believe that this means, because believers are not practicing the law of love (love the Lord your God with all your heart, mind, soul and strength...and your neighbor as yourself), their love will grow cold.

Cold love is ineffective love, or even dead love.

If you find yourself with ineffective or dead love, repent to Him. God is gracious, loving and kind. A "broken and contrite heart" He will not despise. (Psalm 51:17)

Earlier, in the Preface, I mentioned that we need to have true faith and readily recognize true faith in order to avoid being deceived by false prophets, false teachers and false christs. Jesus gave us the key to recognizing the difference between a true believer and a false one. He said in several places, *"Ye shall know them by their fruits."*

Paul warned Timothy about imposters:

"This know also, that in the last days perilous times shall come. For men shall be lovers of their own selves, covetous, boasters, proud, blasphemers, disobedient to parents, unthankful, unholy, without natural affection, trucebreakers, false accusers, incontinent, fierce, despisers of those that are good, traitors, heady, highminded, lovers of pleasures more than lovers of God." 2Timothy 3:1-4

The first characteristic he mentioned was that these false believers would love themselves; the last he mentioned was that they would love pleasure more than God. Let me say it another way: the false believers will love themselves above everyone and everything, including God, and they will seek their own pleasure above that of anyone else, including God's. If in many other ways they look like believers, including the signs and wonders they perform, we will know that if their love for God is not greater than their self-love, and if their love for their neighbors is not at least as great as their love for themselves, we are not to follow them.

Jude, the brother of James, warned believers that men had crept in among them who, in reality, had denied Jesus Christ. Of the many things he said about these men, it is notable that he said they were *"trees whose fruit withereth, without fruit, twice dead, plucked up by the roots."* (1:12) Not only will we know true believers by their fruit, but we will know false believers by their lack of fruit.

Now note how he instructed believers to protect themselves from such deceivers:

"But ye, beloved, building up yourselves on your most holy faith, praying in the Holy Ghost, keep yourselves in the love of God, looking for the mercy of our Lord Jesus Christ unto eternal life." Jude 1:20-21

He said that praying in the Holy Ghost would keep us in the love of God. Does *"keep yourselves in the love of God"* mean we should pray in the Holy Ghost so that God will continue to love us, or does it mean that we are to pray in the Holy Ghost so that we may walk in or be motivated by God's love? It cannot mean the former because, in Romans 8:38-39, Paul confirms that nothing external to the believer can separate us from the love of God, not even false teachers, false prophets and false christs. What the scripture is warning us against is failing to be motivated by the love of God, thus, separating ourselves from God.

Now, lest you think that the fruits that are to identify and be the evidence of true believers are works alone, read what Jesus said in John 13:35: *"By this shall all men know that ye are my disciples, if ye have love one to another."*

Galatians 5:22-25 says, *"But the fruit of the Spirit is love, joy, peace, longsuffering, gentleness, goodness, faith, meekness, temperance: against such there is no law. And they that are Christ's have crucified the flesh with the affections and lusts. If we live in the Spirit, let us also walk in the Spirit."*

Some Christian ministers believe that love is the fruit of the Spirit that contains all the other eight fruits mentioned after it. That may or may not be true, and if it is not, love is certainly the chief fruit of the Spirit. It is this writer's belief that the fruit of the Spirit, combined, equate to holiness, since love assumes obedience to God's Word. All of the fruit of the Spirit named above are facets of the character of the Holy Spirit of God.

The ultimate result of *agape* love at its maturity is the kind of obedience to God that is born out of a pure heart, a heart motivated by love for Him and love for one's neighbors that is equal to the love for oneself. And that is the definition of holiness, because *agape* love is not lip-service affection. It is passion that produces fruit rather than empty promises and pronouncements. Mature love produces true holiness, *"without which no man will see the Lord."(Hebrews 12:14)*

Note that there is another kind of "holiness" that Christians claim, one that is cold and legalistic, devoted first to deeds and compliance rather than first to love. It should be needless to say, that is not the goal Jesus gave us.

Love is the "genesis" gift, the original *modus operandi* of God. It is the beginning and end (goal) of life in Jesus Christ, without which our faith and Christianity are meaningless.

Whatever may stand in the way between you and scriptural faith, identify it and CHANGE.

Submit yourself to God humbly and ask His forgiveness. Ask Him to plant inside you a sincere and burning love for Him and for your neighbors, whether they are across the street or across continents.

Tell Him you want to begin to walk in good works, works that will glorify Him – because you love Him.

Then go to those who have taught you scriptural doctrines that fail to measure up to this standard, and – gently, lovingly and privately – ask them to study out the subjects raised and discussed here, prayerfully before God and with an open Bible.

If ministers of God and the Church in general begin to walk in Biblical faith – i.e., doing God-prescribed works with the motivation of love for Him and love for our neighbors – we will see a dramatic change in our own lives, the lives of our neighbors and the complexion of the country in which we live. We might even usher in revival, which the world and the Church so desperately need.

As it is, the Church is caught up in politics, arguing and creating factions over the great injustices in the world. (Well, of course injustices are in the world! How could they *not* be?)

And the Church has not separated itself from the world. For all the differences that we politick over, we have not completely given up the lusts of the flesh, the lust of the eyes and the pride of life.

We talk about killing our enemies rather than loving them. We are ready to fight and die for the Constitution of the United States, but we will not die, even to our own ideas, for the gospel's sake.

We enter into divorce for the sake of convenience or because we have "fallen out of love" with our spouses. (*Love never fails*. I Corinthians 13:8)

We criticize, judge and reject other believers who do not agree with our doctrines, instead of seeking with them to find the truth of scriptures.

We gossip like unbelievers; verbally attack our leaders, whether Christian or secular; hate our enemies; and complain, instead of praying for solutions.

We are addicted to television and other forms of entertainment as completely as the world is.

We are given to gluttony instead of fasting.

We seem bent on standing firmly against wholehearted trust in God's Word.

And we give our attention to virtually any distraction that happens to fly before us, but we will not give our attention to the Holy Spirit of God.

The question is not *whether* the Church runs to the same excesses as the world, *but to what degree!* We are guilty of saying we have been delivered from sin, but without walking totally away from it. We try to see how close we can get to hell's fire without getting burned, but we avoid the fire of the Holy Spirit as though it would destroy us.

(The fire of the Holy Spirit will destroy fleshly lusts, which destruction we should welcome.)

And as things stand, it is the rare lay Christian, even among so-called evangelicals, who will actually preach the gospel. Why? Because we have abdicated that responsibility to full-time preachers, supposing it is their job instead of ours. Further, we haven't allowed God to totally transform our lives. So we think we have nothing spectacular to offer – even though the gospel itself is spectacular! It is the power of God unto salvation to those who will believe.

Many of the problems in America could be solved if Christians walked consistently in true faith, which means we would obey the great commission of Christ, and we would do it out of the kind of love and power that would compel the hard-hearted to acknowledge Jesus Christ is Savior.

But what have we done instead?

We have preached the gospel of contention and condemnation, especially toward homosexuals, abortion advocates and political enemies. We cannot win them for Christ with hatred toward them. While we hate sin, we cannot cross the line to hating sinners.

Or we have preached nothing at all.

Many times, even the pitiful efforts we have made at preaching the truth have required virtually no change of heart in the hearer.

"Just say this prayer and you will be saved," we say in our congregations.

We make it seem that the "betrothal" to Christ is an act of which converts should be ashamed. "Bow your head, close your eyes and just raise your hand," we say, as though the act did not mean the abandonment of their old lives and the bold declaration that they are no longer of this world.

Why is it so difficult for us to tell the lost that believing in Christ means we must count the cost – both of continuing in sin and of abandoning the old life?

Jesus told the multitudes:

"If any man come to me, and hate not his father, and mother, and wife, and children, and brethren, and sisters, yea, and his own life also, he cannot be my disciple. And whosoever doth not bear his cross, and come after me, cannot be my disciple. For which of you, intending to build a tower, sitteth not down first, and counteth the cost, whether he have sufficient to finish it? Lest haply, after he hath laid the foundation, and is not able to finish it, all that behold it begin to mock him, Saying, This man began to build, and was not able to finish." Luke 14: 26-30

Too many prospective converts sit in our congregations and hear a gospel that requires no death to self, no despising of the old life, no counting of the cost in an honest exchange.

We tell them, "Just believe in Jesus and you'll go to heaven." And we don't even tell them what "believe" means.

However, when the same ones who follow those overly simple injunctions walk back into sin, we say, "Well, I guess they must not have been saved."

How can that be so? After all, we told them, "Just do this and you'll be saved."

The truth cannot be both ways. We cannot tell people to say a prayer in order to be saved, and then, when they turn back to sin, say that they were never saved.

By the same token, how can we say these same people who merely raised a hand or said a prayer were saved if they were not changed? People are fond of believing they are "saved" because they once "confessed Christ," or that they said they believe in Christ. The Bible never indicates salvation comes to a person who claims to believe in Christ yet whose lifestyle gives no evidence of a changed life.

Only God knows how many instant converts turn back to sin simply because we have not discipled them, as Jesus instructed us to do. We convince them to say a prayer, tell them they're saved and then we expect them to grow to maturity without our instruction, care and nurturing and without informing them of the trials and sacrifices ahead.

We cannot tell people that merely repeating a prayer or raising a hand in church will result in a guarantee that they will go to heaven. And by all means, if we have "won" them so haphazardly, we can't throw up our hands if they begin to stray, and write them off as though the salvation experience did not stick.

Are we afraid they will not jump at our "sales pitch" if we tell them the truth about what God expects? Are we afraid our church attendance numbers will drop? Jesus was not afraid to lay out the absolute truth and let the "chips" fall where they may. Why? Because He knew that some were ready to make the exchange and some were not ready at that moment in time. Some did not have ears to hear when He preached, but did later, when Peter preached on the day of Pentecost. We need not be so afraid they will walk away and die without Christ that we rush them into a prayer without telling them the costs. We cannot be afraid to turn people off if we make clear what the exchange really is – receiving eternal life in place of eternal death.

We must tell them what faith in Christ means, that it is not a kind of lip-service belief that allows their hearts and deeds to be far from God, but it is a belief born of love for God so strong and pure that, as we persist in faith, it produces works of love toward others and obedience to His voice. And we have to tell them that the Holy Spirit – and we – will stick with them as long as they are willing to grow into the mature believers God intends for them to be.

Have we never wondered why there is no "Prayer of Salvation" in the Bible? Baptism was the declaration for early believers that they were giving up their old ways of life. And obedience to Christ in love – that is, faith – was the fruit, the substance and evidence that they had done so.

Early believers understood the need to make disciples, and to walk with converts as they entered their new lives.* We have not told the whole story, but substituted a prayer and raised hand for the discipling of converts.

We have to tell them that believing is not intellectual assent. It is not simply acknowledgement, requiring no corresponding action.

We have to tell them that believing is not a legalistic obedience to the call to service. The law of the Spirit is the love of God.

We have to explain the costs so that they can count them correctly. That is, give up your life and way of doing things! Love Him enough to follow His acts and His motive! He gave you love freely by dying. Freely you have received, freely give.

It is true that we all must believe that God raised Jesus from the dead. It is also true that even that statement of faith must produce love that finds expression in acts of faith.

Jesus could have come and preached the gospel, but if He had failed to lay down His life out of love, the gospel would not be a love message. There would be no open door. There would be no power to the gospel without the love, the passion that made it work. Can you see that true faith produces works through love?

On that note, we are not really preaching the full gospel if we are not preaching a faith that produces works through love.

Incorporate this definition of scriptural faith into your daily life.

If you need to repent, do it now.

If you have never been born again, ask God to save you and bring you into His fold, to give you His new life in exchange for your old one. Run to Him. And never go back to your old life.

"If any man is in Christ, he is a new creation. Old things have passed away; behold all things have become new."

*In His Great Commission, Jesus said, "Go ye therefore, and teach all nations, baptizing them in the name of the Father, and of the Son, and of the Holy Ghost." (Matthew 28:19) The Greek word translated "teach" is matheteuo (math-ayt-yoo'-o), meaning to disciple.

CHAPTER TEN

What Faith is NOT

No matter how many legs it might have, a stool with no seat is not a place to rest.

Faith is a place of rest because we trust in the work God has already done for us. It is not a place of doubt, unbelief and fear.

Faith is support. It is absolute trust that God will do what He says He will do.

Not what you *hope* He *might* do in spite of what He said.

And it is certainly not what you fear He might NOT do.

Fear, doubt and unbelief are not to be given a place, a harbor in your heart. They are enemy strongholds and have no place in God's camp.

Unbelief does not know what God said. Doubt knows, but does not trust what He said. And fear is tribute paid in honor of the failure expected by doubt and unbelief. You have no need for detailed definitions for these terms. Just call them faith killers.

I have known people for whom worry is an obligation. They believe that if they do not worry about their children's safety, for example, they are not being good parents. That is an unscriptural tradition handed down from other worriers. When the Bible gives promises of protection, provision and care, the hearing of God's promise must be mixed with faith. When faith has come and trust is placed in God for the fulfillment of the promise, there is no place for fear or worry.

Fear, doubt and unbelief undermine your attempt at or hope for resting upon faith.

There must be a resting place in faith, a place upon which you may comfortably place your expectation and hope. This is not primarily a place of resting for your body, but your soul. As we saw in James 2, your body must participate in the kinds of actions that demonstrate your faith. Your soul must rest. It must cease from the striving that fuels worry and anxiety – which are the seeds of fear.

If God's Word says He will supply all your need, you must cooperate, speaking words that agree and acting in agreement. That will be easy if your soul rests in the knowledge He is doing exactly what He said. But if your soul is anxious, you must examine your heart for doubt and unbelief, confess any to God and set your heart on unwavering trust in Him. The more you love God, the more you will grow to trust Him. Then your acts of agreement will be in concert with your faith. Without the soul rest, your acts of agreement are dead works, works of striving and trying to make faith work.

When you give place to fear, unbelief or doubt, you have removed the "seat" from your three-legged stool of faith. Or clearer still, you have cut the legs off the resting place. Instead, you will be attempting to sit on a different three-legged stool – fear, doubt and unbelief – that has no place for rest. Fear is always a very uncomfortable place to try to live.

Fear cancels your belief. It in fact says, "I don't believe." Fear gives rise to its own acts of obedience – i.e., obedience to fear instead of belief in God's Word. Such a situation is a lack of love for God because fear says He is not trustworthy and/or good.

On the other hand, the three legs of faith – if they are truly in place – will counteract fear, doubt and unbelief. Belief in God's Word affirms that He did say what He is reported to have said, and that the truth of it is unassailable, meaning that it cannot be eroded by time, opinion or circumstances. That stands against and obliterates any fear that you might, somehow, have "got it wrong" or misunderstood it.

Obedience to the Word of God is an act of trust in what God has said. Without acts of obedience, as we have seen before, we cannot be considered to truly trust God's Word. (*"Oh, I believe God, but..."* Notice that "but" reverses "I believe...") By your acts of obedience or trust, you are saying that you refuse to give place to doubt and sin. By acts of disobedience – especially self-willed disobedience – you are saying you refuse to give place to faith in and love of God.

And again, your love for God will be founded on the knowledge of His care for you, His absolute unwillingness to leave you, and the knowledge of His own great love for you.

Perfect love, the apostle John said, casts out all fear. (I John 4:18)

Yet, I have seen people faced with dire crisis whose faith is nonexistent regarding the specific circumstances they are facing. They do not know what God has promised them, so they cannot possibly have faith to overcome the circumstances. They are caught in unbelief. And unless they access God's Word and are able to mix faith with it for victory in their situation, they do not have a leg to stand on. They will fall to the attack of the enemy.

Others may know what God has promised, but have no lifestyle of obedience to His Word, no daily practice of reliance upon Him. The range of the disobedient is broad, including, on one end, those who see how close they can get to sin and still call themselves Christian, and on the other end, people who seem not to know that sin even matters, believing that God's grace gives them the right to live in open disregard for His holy presence. Those in either group, or somewhere in the middle, are on dangerous ground. God does not wink at sin. Playing in Satan's playground comes with a high cost.

The disobedient have deceived themselves. Consequently, while they may think they are strong and secure, they are so weak that the enemy of their souls is easily able to bring the question to them that he used against Eve. "Has God said...?" In other words, he brings doubt about what God really said, what He actually meant, and even whether He truly means what He said. Because they do not have confidence that God reliably keeps His promises, they stumble upon doubt. And disobedience, if it is continued, leads them further from God and His promises with every step.

A daily walk in trust of and communion with God is a must for a life that can readily appropriate the promises He has given.

And then there is the group who knows what God's Word says; they may even know a lot about what it says. But their relationship with Him is so shallow, and their motivation in serving Him has been so superficial, that in a crisis they cannot believe His promises actually apply to them. They have not engaged in a spiritually deep love relationship with their Father. Maybe they have for a time experienced

His day-to-day provision and blessing, but have grown to take Him for granted. Their acts of apparent obedience are likely to be performances for show, motivated by something other than love. God has become an impersonal prayer-answering formula or a panic button for them. Now their lack of love for Him translates, in their own hearts, into a vacuum of His love for them. For them, fear has overcome imperfect love.

What do worried people usually do when they are trapped in unbelief, doubt and fear? They often look for a "Plan B." That is, because they cannot fully trust God they must have an alternate solution.

Because He "might not" supply all their need financially, they may be tempted to resort to borrowing enough money to fix their situation. Or worse, they consider cheating, in order to have more.

Since they may not be very sure He will answer their prayers for healing, they trust doctors first, and medicines, and they keep God in reserve, just in case the doctors and meds don't work.

Such "hybrid faith" has become common in the Church in America. So common that few will dare to suggest it is not a true aspect of faith. That is, trust in medical science is so prevalent that believers have given it the status of faith. To some, that is the only way God heals today. It is as though the Bible instructs them to trust God to work through medicine and medicine alone – even though no such Biblical instruction exists.

When Asa, king of Judah, relied on the king of Syria instead of relying on the Lord for protection against the king of Israel's advances, the prophet told him he had done foolishly, and said, "from henceforth thou shalt have wars." (2 Chronicles 16) Asa was angered and rejected the words of the prophet,. Three years later, scripture notes, he was stricken by disease, and "yet in his disease he sought not to the LORD, but to the physicians." His trust in man's devices and solutions earned Asa reproof by the Lord.

Am I suggesting that believers must stop going to doctors? No. If a person's faith is already invested in and focused on doctors and medicine, nothing good would be accomplished by telling that person to *suddenly* stop trusting medical science if he has not, instead, gained faith in Jesus as Healer. In fact, that would amount to works without faith, which is just as dead as faith without works.

The ideal is faith in Jesus Christ for healing. This author is still reaching forward to the point of placing all his trust in God's promises without reliance on medicine and doctors. It is a worthy goal, but not one to be grasped or leaped into with presumption.

Much has been made in the courts and news media of members in a certain cult that refuse blood transfusions. The reason for their rejection of such things has less to do with any belief God will heal than with a staunch legalistic approach to scriptural injunctions about consuming blood. Nevertheless, the publicity surrounding a number of deaths related to cult members opting out of medical solutions has probably aided in setting a tone of harsh criticism in the media and among the general public against people who do not put their faith in modern medicine. Whatever the reason, faith in God alone for healing is rare today, even frowned upon by some believers.

Let me make it clear that I do not advocate that people with little faith in God's willingness to heal abandon medicine. I do not even advocate that people with great faith in God abandon medicine. People may have strong faith in God for salvation, but having been told that healing is not for today – or similarly, having been told nothing at all about healing – their faith for God to heal them or a loved one may be very weak indeed. If you do not have very strong faith that God will heal you, you would be wise not to pretend to have it. That kind of faith – the kind that is not truly convinced, but causes you to think you should pretend to have it – is not fully formed.

What I do advocate is that people examine the object of their faith to see if it is an object in which the Bible tells us to invest faith. They should know whether theirs is genuine faith or some hybrid that has sprouted from a culture steeped in worldly wisdom. I would hope all believers would begin investing more and more of their trust in God and His Word, and thus, less in the solutions of mankind.

Honesty would require those without faith for finances, healing or some other Biblical promise of provision to simply go to God and say, "Father, I must confess that, for whatever reason, I cannot at this time put all my trust in You to supply this need. I don't adequately understand your Word on the subject, and I have not mixed my hearing of Your Word with faith. Help me to grow beyond this situation, and to learn to trust You explicitly for all my needs."

Examine your faith to know its condition as much as is possible. Then set your heart at having pure Biblical faith, through the Holy Spirit's guidance. But don't try to short-circuit the process. If you will set your heart to believe God for every need and persevere in study and prayer, a time can come when you no longer place faith in doctors, medicine, lenders, the government, your employer or any alternative source for the provision of your needs.

Once others are not your "Plan B" or even primary faith objects, you will be ready to place all your faith in God and His great and many precious promises.

This is very important: don't wait until you encounter a tragedy or some crisis to call upon your faith in God. Begin building your faith before crisis comes. We see in Matthew 7 that storms can come to anyone, so we must build our houses on the rock of God's Word instead of the sand of man's meager abilities.

It may be timely to speak about the future of medical care in America, given a governmental philosophy that is aggressively seeking to cause all citizens to be dependent upon government-controlled health care, and even dependent upon government control of virtually everything. I note that the Bible allows and even ascribes certain roles to government, but health care is not one of them. If you are a person who is currently dependent upon the health care system in America, you might be well advised to begin now changing your focus to one that depends upon the promises of God rather than upon those of politicians.

A word to the wise, as they say, should be sufficient.

If you are trapped in fear that God will abandon you in a pinch, confront the fear. Ask Him to show you the source of such inordinate unscriptural fear.

Likewise, if you recognize that you are plagued with doubt and unbelief about certain aspects of God's promises, don't pretend for the sake of some hyper-faith culture in your church congregation or surroundings that your faith is where it should be.

Now, on the subject of pretending, let me move to a broader aspect of faith than the specific focus of God's provision.

Ananias and Sapphira found themselves amid a church "on fire," a church with pure, unadulterated faith in God, a population of people so committed to faith in God that they sold all their possessions and pooled the proceeds for the common good. Why this couple was not in concert with the moving of the Holy

Spirit in that time we are not told. But whatever the reason, they thought they had to *appear* to be part of what God was doing. That proved fatal for them both.

Was their downfall related to an inordinate desire to be part of a culture, or to *appear* to be a part, without the spiritual sacrifice that brought about the culture? We cannot really say. But if that is the case, are many Christians today very different?

Being a Christian and having faith are not about being part of a social group or belonging to a culture. All of us want to belong, to not be separate from a body of like-minded people. But when that desire takes precedence over a desire to fully belong to God through Jesus Christ, then problems arise.

We hear Christians call themselves by some group name as though they identify with the group more than with Jesus Christ. They are Baptists, Lutherans, Catholics, Presbyterians, Episcopalians, Pentecostals or members of some sect of Christianity. And, certainly, in their midst are those who are more loyal to the group beliefs than to the incorruptible Word of God. The truth of that is visible in the fact that these groups are divided from each other with very little interaction or Christian fellowship. Each considers his group to be the inerrant one, or at least, more acceptable to God and himself than the others.

If you are a true believer in Jesus, you have been joined with God in Christ Jesus. As a consequence, you are a member of the body of Christ, a child of God

– nothing more, nothing less. You have not been joined to a sub-group of Christians.

I have met people who are so committed to the doctrines held by a particular denomination or sect that they cannot receive as a brother or sister in the Lord a true believer from another denomination. That is a perversion of the gospel.

I have met quite a few people who literally thought they were saved because they "joined" a church congregation as a child, but had never actually joined their hearts with God through Jesus Christ.

Let me be clear. The idea that you can join yourself to a group of people – even to a group of Christians – without being fully joined with God in Christ, is a perversion of the gospel. There is no safety in numbers, if that is the underlying motive for giving priority to group membership over Christ membership. You can "join a church" or be a full-fledged member of a denomination and spend eternity in hell if you are not fully joined with Jesus Christ – i.e., joined with God Himself in the body of Christ.

Further, I have met members of cults who were so committed to identification with the beliefs of their group that they could not simply believe plain teachings of the Bible. As with Lot's wife, the culture was more important to them than the clear path of God's directives.

Each of us must stand before God, without the label or the group comfort of a denomination, sect or faction, and give account for what we have done in our earthly lives. It will be useless to say to God in that day that you were a "good _____" [fill in the blank with the name of your particular denomination, sect or cult].

When the Corinthians began to realign themselves and identify with individuals more than with Jesus Christ, Paul asked them, "Is Christ divided? Was Paul crucified for you?" He might well ask some of us today, "Did the Baptist die for you? Did Martin Luther or the Pope die for you? Did the founder of your denomination die for you?"

Paul rightly considered identification with any sub-group of Christians to be division. (I Corinthians 1:10-13) Until we stop seeking to identify with a sub-set of the body of Christ, we will continue hindering the purposes of God in the earth.

Our love for Jesus Christ demands that we shun the sub-categories we append to the title of "Christian."

At best, your identification with a sub-group can keep you from seeing God's perfect will done in your life. At worst, you could be a member in good standing of a group without being a member in right-standing in the body of Christ, and, as such, miss the salvation you so confidently believed you had.

If you find yourself reacting negatively to this talk about the divisiveness of denominations, even though they are extra-biblical, it may be that you have adopted your denomination as a tradition. The subtle nature of traditions makes them seem a part of who you are. Thus, when anyone speaks against a tradition someone has adopted as part of his identity, it is like an attack on that one's "self." Traditions that are dear to our soulish lives – e.g., identification with an *alma mater*, a region of the country, a political party, an ethnic group or even a sports team – can easily become a source of conflict when criticized, fairly or unfairly, because we see ourselves as members of the group under fire.

The clear solution is that we must not have as part of our identity membership in any group other than the Body of Christ. He bought us completely. Our only claim to membership or belonging must be in Him.

Again, faith can come only from the Word of God. Since there is no Biblical support for division in the body of Christ, the existence of denominations and the insistence on identifying with any denomination or sub-group of Christ is an extra-Biblical, hybrid kind of "faith" that takes away from pure fellowship rather than enhancing it.

It should be manifestly clear that, at most, only one group among all denominations and sects of Christianity could hold the pure truth of God, since each may have points of disagreement with the others. And yet, there is no guarantee that any is fully sound when it comes to doctrine.

You might consider that the doctrines of your denomination are more nearly pure than all the rest; in fact, your denomination might be pretty sound doctrinally, but the truth remains: if you did not receive the truth of any doctrine from the conviction of the Holy Spirit – i.e., if, instead, you received it as truth from men without submitting it to the Word of God and the illuminating teaching of the Holy Spirit – you have put your trust in the words of men and, possibly, false doctrines.

We must not be dependent upon human sources for our understanding, but we must rely fully upon the power of the Holy Spirit to teach. Further, we must engage in an honest scriptural examination of any doctrines we have been taught by others. Keep what the Holy Spirit confirms in the scriptures and seek His truth for every other doctrinal question.

Again, there are many fine pastors and teachers both in denominational churches and non-denominational settings. *A dedicated and sincere minister will not be threatened by your desire to confirm the truth of scripture by your own Spirit-led study of God's Word.* No minister should ever feel threatened by a congregant with such a love for truth that he will seek it earnestly on his own, apart from the minister's teaching. That kind of hunger for truth in a believer should be the goal and result of any minister's faithful efforts at preaching the gospel.

In fact, if any minister insists you must believe what he or she says without question, or without verifying it yourself through study of God's Word and prayer, you are definitely listening to the wrong person.

Remember, the Holy Spirit will lead you into all truth. (John 16:13)

I should point out, also, that there are many sincere adherents to false doctrines. Sincerity is no guarantee of righteousness. Likewise, being sincerely wrong is no consolation, and certainly no substitute for the mentoring of the Holy Spirit.

You and I clearly cannot afford to rely on anything other than the leading of the Holy Spirit for our beliefs about scripture, and, by extension, in finding a place of corporate worship. Many pick a congregation because it meets near home or because friends and family members go there, or perhaps they assume it is so big that that many people can't be wrong. Neither is God's way for us to find truth.

This is a call to draw close to the Holy Spirit of God, my friends, to cease the practice of being spoon-fed by ministers and swallowing whole whatever comes from the pulpit because of your love and/or respect for the person speaking. If that minister is committed to the Word of God, he (or she) will be willing to affirm that only the Holy Spirit has the ability to give understanding of truth. (See Jesus's word to Peter in Matthew 16:17) Again, if any minister tells you that you can believe whatever he or she says without the need to confirm it scripturally, run from that person.

Our faith in God is founded upon a relationship with Him through Jesus Christ, not with a denomination or any sub-group of believers. It is a love relationship, at that. And no relationship can thrive on fear, doubt and unbelief...or pretension.

Whenever we see that we fall short of obedience to God, we are told by the gospels and epistles to confess our failure (sin) to God and seek His correction and solutions.

Faith is trust in a reality that natural eyes cannot always affirm beforehand. Yet, a loving knowledge of God, established through the blood of Jesus and God's Word, can open the way to faith that has no fear of failure. But to possess that faith, we must be willing to sever our bonds to worldly wisdom and the solutions of men, and to seek God with all our hearts. If we expect to have such faith, we cannot stop halfway.

Jesus said it this way, *"If any man will come after me, let him deny himself, and take up his cross, and follow me."*

Your cross and my cross amount to a commitment to trust God fully, and to be led by Him regardless of any possible hardship we might encounter.

Not by denominational or man-made doctrines. Not by the teachings of men to the exclusion of the teaching of the Holy Spirit.

Pretty radical, right? The first followers of Christ would be considered radical in many places today, so, being radical, in and of itself, isn't a bad thing.

There are many counterfeit ways of relating to God and His Word that give the appearance of being faith.

Do not settle for anything less than the faith you have seen demonstrated in the Word of God by believers fully committed to Him.

God will not deny you great faith if you are willing to follow Him in pursuing His best.

[*Author's note: I am sure that many will be tempted at this point to take offense at the foregoing stance with regard to denominations and sub-groups of Christianity. However, you and I must take our stand on the Word of God rather than on the commonly accepted traditions or practices we see in the Christian culture. Just because the majority of believers in the country may accept denominations and divisions in the body of Christ does not make them valid or pleasing to God. And being pleasing to God is the object of faith. Our allegiance must be to what His Word directs rather than to what the culture displays.*]

CHAPTER ELEVEN

The Highest Forms of Faith

Let's sum it up.

How can you begin to walk in such an elevated, impossible-sounding faith? First, think back to some of the things Jesus said about conversion. For example:

"Verily I say unto you, Except ye be converted, and become as little children, ye shall not enter into the kingdom of heaven. Whosoever therefore shall humble himself as this little child, the same is greatest in the kingdom of heaven." Matthew 18:3-4

"But I say unto you, Love your enemies, bless them that curse you, do good to them that hate you, and pray for them which despitefully use you, and persecute you; That ye may be the children of your Father which is in heaven: for he maketh his sun to rise on the evil and on the good, and sendeth rain on the just and on the unjust. For if ye love them which love you, what reward have ye? do not even the publicans the same? And if ye salute your brethren only, what do ye more than others? do not even the publicans so? Be ye therefore perfect, even as your Father which is in heaven is perfect." Matthew 5:44-48

You can only reach such an elevated state of spirituality by becoming humble. A sapling may be bent and shaped, but a full-grown tree cannot be bent and shaped without being destroyed. Likewise, a very young child may be molded and taught, but it is far more difficult once a degree of self-direction has taken hold.

Can we return to the teachability of heart that Jesus wants, a teachability that is exemplified by young children? Even if we have already been molded and shaped by years of self-direction? Absolutely, if we are born again by the Spirit of God and allow Him to do the work in our hearts that He wants to do. Not only can we, we must.

Jesus "*took upon Himself the form of a servant,*" said Paul in the book of Philippians (also see Luke 22:27). When He washed the disciples' feet, He told them He did it as an example to them, that they (we) should not try to be greater than He. (John 13:16)

"*But he that is greatest among you shall be your servant. And whosoever shall exalt himself shall be abased; and he that shall humble himself shall be exalted.*" Matthew 22:11-12

Paul asked, "*And what do you have that you did not receive?*" (I Corinthians 4:7b) The answer, of course, is NOTHING. We have received everything that we own. So, then, Jesus would say to you and me, "*Freely you have received, freely give.*" (Matthew 10:8)

Perform an inventory of all that God has given you.

He has provided you with the gift of eternal life.

Has he given you healing, food, shelter, clothing, water, hope, forgiveness, comfort, kindness, patience, love?

We need not walk very far to find someone who needs one or all of the above.

You can never repay the debt you owe to Him. He gave everything to us freely, which implies no debt is owed. Yet it is written in Romans (13:8) that we do owe a debt of love: "*Owe no man any thing, but to love one another: for he that loves another has fulfilled the law.*"

Therefore, consider your debt to God as payable to others, wherever you find them in need.

Godly giving is not just money, though it does include that. You may have heard one minister or another say something like this: "Show me your wallet and your calendar, and I'll show you your priorities in life."

It is true; we make time for and spend money on the things that are important to us. (Yes, that should include your family members, but not be exclusively them.)

"*But whoso hath this world's good, and seeth his brother have need, and shutteth up his bowels of compassion from him, how dwelleth the love of God in him?*" I John 3:17

"Greater love has no one than this, that a man lay down his life for his friends." John 15:13

When we give compassionately – of time, money, forgiveness, food, water, the gospel, whatever is needed – to help the hurting and the lost, we are walking wonderfully close to the heart of God.

When we shun these, we are walking dangerously close to the broad way of destruction.

People – Christians as well as non-Christians – give for many reasons, including for the purpose of receiving wealth, as has been the focus of so many popular ministers over recent decades. But if the primary motivation for giving is not love for God and love for our neighbors – *agape* love as described in I Corinthians 13 – the giving is merely sounding brass and tinkling cymbals.

Let me clarify that statement for those of us who have been caught up in the "prosperity" gospel.

If we give in order to get rich rather than because we love God and our neighbors, our giving is an empty self-centered act that amounts to sounding brass and tinkling cymbals. Our acts and "good" deeds amount to nothing unless love is at their center. (I Corinthians 13:1-3)

I'm not saying it is wrong to expect God will return blessings to you when you give to others. His Word affirms that He will. I'm speaking of the motivation by which you give. If your motive in giving is to make yourself wealthy, you should re-examine your heart.

It remains that the greatest gift we have received is eternal life through Jesus Christ. Of all that we are to give freely, salvation is the most urgent and important. We have it to give, we are commissioned to give it, and by the power of the Holy Spirit, we are equipped to give it. Nothing should hold us back from finding those who are lost and giving them the love and truth that God has given us through Jesus Christ. If you find yourself insecure in your knowledge of God's Word regarding salvation, then you must make it your purpose to learn the gospel message and how to share it with the lost. Set your heart to learning that, and ask the Holy Spirit to teach you how to win souls. (He is your Teacher, after all.)

And if the message of this book is not yet completely clear, let me clarify this one point: When you share the gospel message, it is absolutely necessary to be motivated by your love for God and for the lost. The Word of God is powerful and sharper than any two-edged sword. But remember that faith works by love. You may be the most eloquent preacher known, but if you preach to prove a point, to "wow" an audience, to vanquish someone's theological stance, to gain God's favor, instill a sense of guilt or condemnation, to manipulate or show off your intellectual prowess or insight into the things of God – for any reason other than the pure love of God for a hurting soul – you will not be doing what is pleasing to God.

Love transports the Word of God into the deepest parts of a hearer's soul. The Psalmist says, "*Deep calls unto deep...*" (Ps. 42:7) I believe one meaning of that reference is that in order to reach the innermost parts of someone's heart, another must communicate from the innermost part of his own heart – deep unto deep. A heart filled with love speaking to a heart with an empty place created for the same. Just as water finds its own level, love finds its own designated place once it begins to flow.

God does that to us. He wraps His Truth in love and sends it to us through many various means, using the open window of our souls at the opportune moment.

Somehow, the lost can often only hear God's voice when their hearts have been ripped open by tragedy or loss, or when their hearts have been prepared by another's intercessory prayer. Make sure your communication with them is steeped in God's compassion and love. It is then that the Spirit of God can truly communicate – His deep unto theirs.

How much better if we take the Word to them in love *before* they encounter tragedy or trial!

Love is the necessary motive for all that we do. The Word of God is the source of all true faith. And obedience to the Word, in love, is the call of God for our lives.

What does this mean in practical terms? It means that when you encounter a person who rubs you wrong, who hates you or whom you dislike, you must begin to ask God to give you His love for that person. It means the politician you think is despicable and tainted with evil is worthy of your time in prayer, not because he or she deserves it, but because God said we are to love our enemies. Our debt to Him, we owe to them. We should always keep in mind that we do not deserve the grace God has given us in opening our eyes to truth.

College students, business men and women, the elderly in nursing homes, the harried physician, the truck driver stuck in traffic, the woman whose husband has just left her, the soldier sitting on his helmet thousands of miles from home – people everywhere deal with peculiar situations that seem to warrant the occasional attitude of not wanting to show grace to the easily unlovable. In certain such moments, obedience to the Holy Spirit seems to be impossible. But we must remember, the impossible is only a self-denying and cross-bearing breath away.

Love is not just a good idea. It is the "silver bullet" for your neighbor's fears and doubts. That is, God's love through you is the answer. And it's God's commandment. He commands it because He has made His love freely available to you and me.

As we saw in the previous chapter, Jude has the answer to keeping yourself in the love of God.

"But ye, beloved, building up yourselves on your most holy faith, praying in the Holy Ghost, keep

yourselves in the love of God, looking for the mercy of our Lord Jesus Christ unto eternal life." Jude 1:20-21

Scripture instructs us to be baptized in the Holy Spirit and to be filled with the Holy Spirit. You know that God is love, but have you also considered that that means Jesus and the Holy Spirit are, in essence, also love? When we are filled with the presence of the Holy Spirit, how can we NOT be filled with the love of God – which is the leading fruit of the Holy Spirit, according to Galatians 5? And having the fullness of His love in us and around us, we may assure ourselves of remaining in His love by praying in the Holy Ghost.

Now let us ask ourselves if we are truly obeying God. That is, are we truly walking in faith?

Do we truly believe?

Many still may answer quickly, based on what they hope faith means, still resisting the truth about faith. We know that some will not examine their hearts, assuming that they are "all right." We know from the scriptures we've seen that some will *"see, and not perceive; and ... hear, and not understand."* (Mark 4:12)

But it is hoped that some who currently take belief for granted will awaken at the clarity of God's commandment to believe in such a way that love for God and for our fellow man leads us to do His will.

It is hoped many will see that the faith God calls us to is not simplistic belief. It is a composite with three components – a three-legged stool, if you will – that may be understood easily when viewed with childlike trust, and practiced when obedience is achieved through complete trust in Almighty God.

Those inclined to ignore the fixed link between faith, love and works (obedience) might be susceptible to the deceptive idea that they may love God without knowing or obeying His Word. They might falsely believe they can be obedient to His will without overt love for Him that shows up in humility, heart-felt worship, sharing the gospel with the lost and giving of their time and money to His purposes. They might think that all God expects of them is a wink and a nod on Sunday, an acknowledgement that He exists, and an admission that they "believe in Jesus."

Read Matthew 25 again and see what Jesus expects of His followers.

"For I was an hungered, and ye gave me meat: I was thirsty, and ye gave me drink: I was a stranger, and ye took me in: Naked, and ye clothed me: I was sick, and ye visited me: I was in prison, and ye came unto me."

Decide now that you will be a believer who demonstrates your love for God and your neighbors. Do not miss the mark by presuming you have no need to compare your faith with the kind God has prescribed.

As Christians, we should be asking ourselves two questions with regard to our thoughts, decisions and actions:

Is this thought or action an expression of my love for God?

Is it an expression of my love for my neighbor(s)?

As we grow in the knowledge of God through Jesus Christ, more and more our answers to those questions should be yes.

Ask yourself this question daily: *How have I demonstrated the love of God to the lost and hurting today*? If you cannot answer, ask God to fill you with His love for those to whom He wants you to minister.

What is the consequence of not having genuine faith? Do we really need to ask that question?

Even though it is not a pleasant subject, we do need to address reality.

The consequence for failing to have genuine faith toward God through Jesus Christ is the same consequence as for rejecting Jesus Christ.

Eternal torment.

Hell is not a gimmick dreamed up by imaginative preachers; it is the very real and tragic consequence of rejecting God's terms for salvation. It is agonizing pain and torture without let-up. No reprieve, pardon or parole. The sentence can never be commuted.

Here are a few of the many scriptural references to eternal damnation:

"...fear not them which kill the body, but are not able to kill the soul: but rather fear him which is able to destroy both soul and body in hell." Matthew 10:28

"The Son of man shall send forth his angels, and they shall gather out of his kingdom all things that offend, and them which do iniquity; And shall cast them into a furnace of fire: there shall be wailing and gnashing of teeth." Matthew 13:41-42

"Then said the king to the servants, Bind him hand and foot, and take him away, and cast him into outer darkness; there shall be weeping and gnashing of teeth." Matthew 22:13

"And cast ye the unprofitable servant into outer darkness: there shall be weeping and gnashing of teeth." Matthew 25:30

"Then shall he say also unto them on the left hand, Depart from me, ye cursed, into everlasting fire, prepared for the devil and his angels:... And these shall go away into everlasting punishment: but the righteous into life eternal." Matthew 25:41, 46

"... the Lord Jesus shall be revealed from heaven with his mighty angels, In flaming fire taking vengeance on them that know not God, and that obey not the gospel of our Lord Jesus Christ: Who shall be punished with everlasting destruction from the

presence of the Lord, and from the glory of his power." 2 Thessalonians 1:7-9

Hell is not a viable alternative to living for Jesus Christ. No third route exists between heaven and hell. The only route by-passing hell goes straight through Jesus Christ.

He has purchased us body, soul and spirit – if indeed we have trusted Jesus Christ as our Savior. If we claim to have been crucified with Christ, we must ask ourselves this: if we died with Him, of what good is our old life and old way of doing things?

The answer, of course, is: Absolutely no good.

Jesus has a question of His own to ask us, a startling one: *"Nevertheless, when the Son of man cometh, shall He find faith on the earth?"* Luke 18:8

If you ask Him for the impossible love that He makes eminently possible, and if you receive it and continue in it, He will find faith in you when you stand before Him. After all, it is written, *"Ask and you shall receive."*

Dismiss your preconceived notions about faith and give your heart completely to His guidance.

Faith by itself is a one-legged stool. Faith with acts of rote obedience still wavers only on two legs. But when your faith is motivated by love for God and love for your neighbors, it suddenly gains stability to stand on any terrain.

"And thou shalt love the Lord thy God with all thy heart, and with all thy soul, and with all thy mind, and with all thy strength: this is the first commandment. And the second is like, namely this, Thou shalt love thy neighbor as thyself. There is none other commandment greater than these." Mark 12:30-31

CHAPTER TWELVE

The Sharing of Faith

Finally, here is a definition of faith you may never have considered before.

Faith is God's means of sharing Himself with us. It is His way of giving humans a small portion of the power, understanding, wisdom and character that is His alone.

His power is infinite. His love is boundless. His grace is indescribable. His patience is longer than our imaginations can grasp. And His promises to bestow these, and more, upon us are so magnanimous we often fail to consider they are actually true.

Yet, God has ordained that, through our trust in Him and His revealed word – meaning the incarnate Word, Jesus Christ, as well as the spoken and written Word, the Holy Bible – we appropriate God Himself. That is, through these, He allows us to share in His eternal life, He makes available the fruit of the Holy Spirit, which are aspects of the character of God Himself, and He shares with us His power, which makes all things possible. *To those who believe.*

Get the depth of this! Genuine faith is a sharing of God. It is His means of sharing Himself with us.

You and I cannot accept this fully until we know Him more deeply. We cannot "manufacture" the kind of faith that displays the power and character of God seen in the lives of the apostles and disciples in the New Testament, and in the lives of the patriarchs and prophets of the Old Testament. It comes through knowledge of Him, through living in His presence.

And those come through a great abiding love for Him.

So, you see, the history of God's dealings with man has come full circle.

It began in the Garden of Eden with one human in the close, intimate presence of God, and one commandment for that human to obey.

He has brought you to the same circumstance.

You, face to face with the God of the universe, the only intermediary being Jesus Christ Himself. And one simple commandment: love Him without restraint or limit and love your neighbors as yourself.

Everything depends upon how you relate to Him in His presence, how you love, honor and obey Him. The commandment – love Him with all your heart, mind, soul and strength, and love your neighbor as yourself – has two parts that are inextricably bonded, for if you truly love Him, you will also love your neighbor.

Instead of the Garden, we abide with Him in His kingdom.

When you love Him you will want to spend time in His presence. When you spend time with Him you will grow to know Him. When you know Him you will have faith in Him. And when you love and have faith in Him you will obey Him.

Partake of the Tree of Life. Forsake the tree of the knowledge of good and evil, which is the love of the world and of sin.

If you are not quite able to hear this at this moment in your life, hold on to it. Meditate on it. Ask God to usher you into a relationship with Him that begins to plumb more of who He truly is.

Accept what He offers you through His Word and the indwelling of the Holy Spirit.

The greatest offering imaginable is the grace to know God Himself.

Untold numbers of wealthy men –men who have amassed incalculable fortunes – have died without Him, and thus, exchanged their lives for a few trinkets, a few moments of pleasure and an eternity of pain and torturous regret.

But the fundamental things every human truly searches for (and never finds in the ways of the world) – love, joy, peace, patience, gentleness, goodness, faithfulness, temperance and meekness – are found in Him.

Do not waste time with the cares of this world, the lust for other things and the deceitfulness of riches. Go after knowing Him with all your heart.

He expects the impossible of you and me.

Impossible love, impossible works and impossible faith. (Impossible for man, that is.)

They are all made possible by being in His presence and trusting Him to give you what no human can manufacture.

The life of faith is a life of losing yourself in Him.

And whenever you don't seem to have the impossible love, impossible works and impossible faith, remember James 4:2: "*ye have not, because ye ask not.*" Ask and you shall receive.

ABOUT PATRICK MCWHORTER

On graduation from the University of Georgia with a
bachelor's degree in Journalism, Patrick McWhorter
worked as an advertising copywriter and advertising
manager for advertising agencies and corporations for
more than thirty years. He recently retired as a senior
account executive with an advertising and public
relations agency in Georgia. A Vietnam veteran,
Patrick owns and operates a small business with his
wife, and writes Christian novels as time permits. He
and his wife, Laurie, live in Flowery Branch, Ga. They
have two adult sons.

Made in the USA
San Bernardino, CA
18 March 2017